THE 3- HOUR DIET™ for TEENS

Lose Weight and Feel Great in Two Weeks!

Praise for Jorge Cruise's
The 3-Hour Diet™

"Feel like pasta for dinner? Not a problem. Some toast with those eggs? Bring it on. With Jorge's 3-Hour Diet™, eating great and losing weight has never been this simple."

—Jacqui Stafford, *Shape* magazine

"Jorge Cruise has identified a fundamental tenet of successful weight loss—that how you eat is just as important as what you eat. His 3-Hour Diet™ is easy to understand, simple to follow, and specifically designed for those who don't have time to diet. In short, his book is an essential tool for those seeking lifelong weight loss and maintenance."

—Lisa Sanders, MD, Yale University School of Medicine, and author of *The Perfect Fit Diet*

"The 3-Hour Diet™ offers a simple nutrition prescription: how often and how much to control your hunger, *enjoy your food*, and *improve your health*. You can't get much better than that!"

—Leslie Bonci, MPH, RD, LDN, director of sports medicine nutrition, University of Pittsburgh Medical Center, and nutritionist for the Pittsburgh Steelers

"At last, the book to rival the Atkins and South Beach diets is here. If you want to lose weight and keep it off, without giving up any of the food groups, this is the book!"

—John Robbins, author of *Diet for a New America* and *The Food Revolution*

"Jorge has dedicated his life to showing people they can lose weight safely, and this book provides them with the skills to keep the weight off for life. It's a great plan and an inspiring book."

—Kathleen Daelemans, author of *Cooking Thin with Chef Kathleen* and *Getting Thin and Loving Food!*

"Jorge Cruise brings a new dimension to the world of weight loss—empowering and giving you the tools to lose weight by making simple changes in how and when you eat. This technique can help make all the difference."

—Fred Pescatore, MD, author of *The Hamptons Diet* and former associate medical director at the Atkins Center

"Jorge Cruise will keep you looking and feeling your best."

—David Kirsch, author of *The Ultimate New York Body Plan*

"Jorge's 3-Hour Diet™ offers a sound and practical eating plan. His easy-to-follow guide will help any follower see immediate body transformations with long-lasting results."

—Tammy Lakatos Shames and Lyssie Lakatos, RD, LD, CDN, authors of *Fire Up Your Metabolism*

"Wow! I learned a lot from Jorge's fascinating new book. I can easily see how people who follow the 3-Hour Diet™ can shed pounds by keeping their fat-burning metabolism revved up."

—Lucy Beale, author of *The Complete Idiot's Guide to Weight Loss*

"An easy alternative to low-carb, high-fat, or other diets that can have harmful side effects."

—Dale Eustace, PhD, professor of cereal technology, Kansas State University

"This simple, easy-to-understand book gives you practical ideas that you can use immediately to lose weight without feeling hungry, without counting calories, and without feeling deprived in any way. I suggest you get one copy for yourself and one for a friend so you can enjoy the process together."

—Christopher Guerriero, founder and chairman of the National Metabolic and Longevity Research Center, and author of *Maximize Your Metabolism*

"It's refreshing to hear a popular weight-loss guru pan low-carb and other fad diets and tell people the truth: that they can eat anything in moderation. The plan is nutritionally balanced, smart, and practical. The tone is encouraging and forgiving."

—Janis Jibrin, MS, RD, writer for GoodHousekeeping.com, and author of *The Unofficial Guide to Dieting Safely*

"The 3-Hour Diet™ will help millions lose weight and feel great! Eating healthy foods every three hours can help stabilize blood-sugar levels, stave off hunger, and melt away unwanted pounds."

—Jay Robb, certified clinical nutritionist and author of *The Fat Burning Diet*

"Jorge does a great job of creating a straightforward, easy-to-follow eating plan that does not sound like a prison sentence! No restricting carbs, no exotic supplements, and no complex math calculations to make before every meal. The 3-Hour Diet™ is easy to read and simple to follow!"

—Harley Pasternak MSc, celebrity trainer, and author of *Five Factor Fitness*

"The goal in life is to get more done in less time, and Jorge Cruise teaches you how to lose the weight you want in a healthy, safe way in *The 3-Hour Diet*™. What could be better? This is a book that can get you to your physical fitness goal in the shortest, easiest, best way ever."

—Mark Victor Hansen, cocreator, #1 *New York Times* **bestselling series** *Chicken Soup for the Soul*®, **coauthor,** *The One Minute Millionaire*

THE 3-

Collins

An Imprint of HarperCollins*Publishers*

HOUR DIET™
for TEENS

Lose Weight and Feel Great in Two Weeks!

New York Times
Bestselling Author and
AOL Weight Loss Coach

Jorge Cruise

TRADEMARKS:

Jorge Cruise	3-Hour Diet™
8 Minutes in the Morning	3-Hour Plate™
Time Based Nutrition	JorgeCruise.com
Instant Control	3HourDiet.com

OTHER BOOKS BY JORGE CRUISE:

The 3-Hour Diet™	8 Minutes in the Morning for Extra-Easy Weight Loss
The 3-Hour Diet™ on the Go	
8 Minutes in the Morning	8 Minutes in the Morning to a Flat Belly
The 3-Hour Diet™ Cookbook	8 Minutes in the Morning to Lean Hips and Thin Thighs

The 3-Hour Diet™ for Teens

Library of Congress Cataloging-in-Publication Data is available.

ISBN-10: 0-06-117143-3 — ISBN-13: 978-0-06-117143-7

Design by Charles Yuen

❖

First Edition

-wtwo

1. Reducing diets -
2. Weight loss -
3. Physical fitness

"In *The 3-Hour Diet™ for Teens,* Jorge serves up his signature blend of understanding, caring, practicality, and optimism. Talking to teens from a 'been there, done that—and you can, too!' perspective, Jorge is a terrific guide toward weight control, better health—and better self. I am delighted another generation can now claim as its own the sensible guidance Jorge Cruise is uniquely qualified to offer."

—David L. Katz, MD, MPH, FACPM, FACP
Director, Yale Prevention Research Center
Yale University School of Medicine
Medical contributor, *ABC News*
Nutrition columnist, *O, The Oprah Magazine*
www.davidkatzmd.com

"*The 3-Hour Diet™ for Teens* can lead to healthier eating overall and better weight control. The whole family should eat this way!"

Deborah Kennedy, PhD, CNS
Vice President,
Turn the Tide Foundation: Reversing the Obesity Trend
Associate Director of Nutrition,
Yale-Griffin Prevention Research Center

CONTENTS

TO MY TWO SONS, PARKER AND OWEN.

YOU BOTH ARE THE REASON I WROTE THIS BOOK.

I LOVE YOU WITH ALL MY HEART.

ACKNOWLEDGMENTS

Special thanks

To my beautiful wife, Heather. She is the single most important woman who has helped me become the man I am today. Thank you for bringing so much to my life. I am so grateful I have you in my life, doll.

Then a big thank-you to my two sons: Parker and Owen. You both have made my life complete. You bring new joy, happiness, and excitement to me every day. You are the inspiration for this book, and I love you both with all my heart.

To my team at my office who support my dream and vision of empowering America with the 3HourDiet.com center. Thanks to Trixie Kennedy, Chad Wagner, Oliver Stephenson, Jared Davis, and Gretchen Lees. A very special thank-you to Auriana Albert, my content assistant, for helping me refine this book.

Thank you to Tyra Banks for your belief in my work with teens. Also a big thanks for everyone at the *Tyra Banks Show* and Telepictures Productions: Hilary Estey McLoughlin, Cathy Chermol, John Redmann, Shela Bouttier, and Alex Duda. I look forward to working with you all for many years to come.

To Dr. David Katz for all his support and efforts through the years. Your work is vital for the world, and I am so thankful for your friendship. Learn more about Dr. Katz's extraordinary work at www.davidkatzmd.com. Also a special thank-you to Debbie Kennedy, PhD, for her efforts and support with this book. You both are the best.

To the amazing crew at HarperCollins: Jane Friedman, Brian Murray, Joe Tessitore, Kathryn Huck, Kate Jackson, Toni Markiet, and Catherine Onder. Thank you for believing in this book and all the work you put into getting it out to the public.

A big thank-you to all my 3HourDiet.com online clients for their feedback on this book as well as to the wonderful teens who helped me with this book: Doug Gleicher, Ronika Vaughn, Dakotah Blue Rice, Cassandra Cruz, Able Richardson, Molly Super, Chionna Reeves, and Angelica Carlos.

Dear Friend,

If you're holding *The 3-Hour Diet*™ *for Teens* in your hand right now, I bet that you're like me. I struggled with my weight as a teenager and a young man. So I know exactly what it feels like to be overweight. It's *not* fun.

But the good news is that you can change all that by doing one simple thing—learning the power of timing. That's what this book will help you do. And you won't have to give up your favorite foods or going out to eat with your friends. It's the perfect plan for your busy teen lifestyle.

So, what do you do right now?

1. **Read this book!** I was surprised to learn that a lot of people don't actually read the books they buy. Don't be one of those people! If you're pressed for time, jump straight to chapters 3 and 6—they're the most important ones. But I encourage you to read the rest of the book, too. There's some good stuff in there to help you get healthy.

2. **Give your parents the tear-out letter for them in the back of the book.** If you can get your parents involved in your weight loss, you're much more likely to be successful. It's important for them to understand what you're about to do. You will benefit from their support.

3. **Live the 3-Hour Diet™.** I created a special fourteen-day plan for you that will jump-start your success. You'll find it in chapter 8. Start that plan right away.

I want to congratulate you on starting the most exciting journey of your life. Your health is the most precious resource you have to make your future extraordinary. I've met too many teens who've had their confidence destroyed by their unfit and unhealthy bodies. You can change all of that with what's in this book. I *know* you can do it!

You can contact me any time on my website at www.3HourDiet.com. I look forward to seeing your success story on the site with all the others.

Let's get started.

JORGE CRUISE

Jorge Cruise

PART I
INTRODUCTION

THE SECRET TO YOUR BEST BODY

The number of overweight teens in the United States has tripled since the 1970s. According to the Centers for Disease Control and Prevention, 15 percent of American teenagers are overweight or obese. Bottom line: more teens today are physically unfit than at any other time in history.

If you are a teen reading this book, then you most likely already know how feeling unfit and fat can affect your life. I sure do. I struggled with my weight throughout my teen years. I was made fun of and always felt like a misfit. Does that sounds familiar? Not only do you probably hate the jokes, but you may also feel tired and out of breath a lot of the time. Simple tasks like walking between classes or cleaning your room exhaust you. As a young adult, you should have energy to spare, but if you're overweight you might feel like you're a hundred years old.

Well, that's all about to change. This book will show you how to achieve your *best body*—get slim, fit, and energetic—and keep it for the rest of your life. You see, developing good habits now that you maintain as you grow up will set the *foundation* that will keep you energetic and happy, and give you a better chance to help prevent diseases like diabetes or cancer. You'll have the freedom to move freely through the world, unburdened by excess weight or low self-image. And you'll develop the skills to achieve any goal you set your mind to.

The 3-Hour Diet™ is about empowering you to take control of your health and your life. I challenge you, therefore, to read this chapter right now.

When you start living the 3-Hour Diet™, you'll be amazed at how easy the plan is to follow and how great you'll feel. Right off the bat, you could lose up to two pounds every week. This kind of slow, steady weight loss is recommended by doctors as the healthiest way to lose weight, because you're more likely to keep it off if you lose it slowly. If you go on a crash diet (drastically cutting calories to an unhealthy level) and lose a lot of weight in a short amount of time, you'll just gain it right back—and then some—when you start eating normally again. We're talking about changing your whole lifestyle to make sure that this weight stays off for the rest of your life. That's how you'll achieve your best body.

As you start the 3-Hour Diet™, one of the most immediate changes you'll notice is a dramatic increase in your energy level. If you're overweight, you know how you feel tired and worn out and don't have the energy to play sports or ride your bike? When people try to lose weight, they often skip meals, thinking that if they just stop eating they'll become skinny. Well, it's doesn't work like that. When you skip meals, your blood sugar drops quickly, which causes your energy level to drop. You can't think clearly and all you want to do is take a nap. When you eat every three hours, however, you keep your blood-sugar level stable and provide a steady flow of fuel to your muscles and brain. We'll discuss this more later on, but for now remember that eating every three hours steadies your mood and boosts your energy levels. You'll have a steady source of energy to keep you going all day long.

Finally, when you start feeling more energetic and seeing those two pounds disappear every week, your self-esteem will skyrocket. When your clothes start feeling too loose instead of too tight and you have to go shopping for smaller sizes, you'll start feeling really good about yourself. When you finally have the energy to go hiking with your friends or go for a long bike ride, you'll feel so proud of your accomplishments! When you learn to control your appetite by eating every three hours, you'll feel strong, confident, and empowered by your new lifestyle. You'll be surprised at how this will affect other areas of your life, too. You'll walk taller and straighter. You'll feel confident when you meet new people and look them in the eye as you shake their hands. You'll feel comfortable wearing shorts or skirts instead of covering yourself up. You'll like the new healthier you so much that you'll want to continue treating yourself well for the rest of your life.

The Power of Eating Every Three Hours

So now you know that the 3-Hour Diet™ will help you lose weight, give you more energy, and boost your confidence. But how can eating every 3 hours change your life so dramatically? What does timing have to do with losing weight? **Well, timing has *everything* to do with losing weight.**

Here's how it works.

The 3-Hour Plan

The most important thing to remember is that eating every 3 hours will help you manage your blood-sugar level so that you control your appetite. When your appetite is under control, you won't binge or overeat. When you control your appetite, you control your weight and *you control your life*. And best of all, there are no restrictions, no counting calories, and no banned foods. The second part of the book (chapters 3 through 6) is dedicated to giving you all the secrets to doing the 3-Hour Diet™ successfully.

Why I Wrote This Book

You might be thinking to yourself, "Jorge has probably never really been fat. This guy has always been trim and lean. Right?" The answer is no. I used to be an overweight kid and young man.

I know firsthand what it's like to feel embarrassed by extra weight. I've been there. My dad and sister have been there, too. At one time, we were all fat and unhealthy.

Jorge lost 34 pounds in 17 weeks; you can, too!

I grew up in a house where everybody ate large portions. I probably ate enough food to feed three kids. I got so chubby that my mom used to call me *el rey* ("the king" in Spanish). But the kids at school called me other names like "lardass" and "fatso." By the time I was fifteen, I was not only fat, I had frequent headaches, asthma, stomach problems, and other issues. I was a mess.

Because of my weight and other physical problems, I could never keep up with the other kids in gym class. When we had to run the mile, the other students all passed me by as I huffed and puffed. I felt so heavy and slow. Most of all, I felt embarrassed. I couldn't do one push-up or pull-up. I couldn't even do a push-up with my knees on the floor. I know what it's like to feel humiliated by my body.

When I was a teenager, two life-altering events forced me to take stock of my weight and my health—my appendix burst and my dad was diagnosed with prostate cancer. I resolved to focus on improving my health and fitness.

I tried every fad diet on the market to lose weight, probably like you have. But every diet failed me. That's what led me to a career in diet and fitness. I created the 3-Hour Diet™ because none of the existing plans helped control my hunger. In addition to the diet, I incorporated just a few minutes each day of strength training to build muscle and burn more fat. My eating and exercise plan is so simple and easy that I am able to stick to it, even now that I'm married, a dad with two little boys, and run the 3HourDiet.com weight control center.

I still have a scar on my right side to remind me of how lucky I am to be alive—and of my determination to stay healthy. Today I am a busy man. But I have kept the weight off. I still eat every three hours. My enthusiasm for weight control has inspired the rest of my family to get healthy, too. They stay slim by paying careful attention to when they eat.

So I speak from experience when I say that *your health is your most valuable asset.* Protecting your health will empower you to follow your dreams and achieve your goals—just as it did for me. I challenge you to start your journey toward a healthy new you. This book is the first step on your way to a healthy body and a positive future.

And there is one other reason why I wrote this book. About a year ago I meet a wonderful lady who inspired me to reach out to teens. Her name is Tyra Banks. Tyra is America's top model, and I am very lucky to call her my good friend. She is the one I have to thank for connecting me to millions of teens in America. As the *Tyra Banks Show*'s diet and fitness coach, I coached an amazing group of teens whom you will meet in chapter 6. They'll share some of their secrets to doing the diet successfully.

So before we continue, here's what you need to remember: When you learn to eat every 3 hours, you will gain control over your blood sugar, which will help put you in control of your appetite. When you control your appetite, you control your weight. When you control your weight, you'll feel so much more energized and confident. Your self-esteem will go through the roof. You'll enjoy looking at yourself in the mirror and appreciating all the hard work you've done. You'll feel so good about yourself, so healthy and fit, that nothing will stand in your way. You'll be able to achieve any goal you set for yourself.

Let's get started!

THE PROBLEM

I was teased a lot in school. You would think that people in high school will be more mature and it will be a better experience than junior high, but mine wasn't. I would hear other kids snicker behind me, and I would just ignore it. But the third week into school I was walking out to leave and these kids were throwing rocks at me. That day I decided to quit school.

—Molly

Molly, one of the teens in my group from the *Tyra Banks Show*, has lost 15 pounds so far! Does her story sound familiar to you? Do you feel like they're snickering behind your back when you walk to class? Or are they more obviously mean by throwing rocks or poking at you? As I mentioned in chapter 1, statistics tell us that close to 15 percent of teenagers in the United States are overweight or obese. That's about one in six kids! So even though it might seem like you're the only one in your family, school, or neighborhood who is overweight, you're not. It's important to remember that.

In this book you'll learn from kids all over the country who have experienced the same cruelty from their peers, the same frustration from their parents, the same embarrassment in gym class, and the same awkwardness when buying clothes as you have. **You're not alone.** Kids all over America understand where you're coming from. I understand where you're coming from. I know how sad, lonely, and desperate you might be feeling. **We're going to change all that** *forever*. By using and living the 3-Hour Diet™, you're going to join my weight-loss family where no one judges you, people understand you, and everyone is there to help you succeed. For this plan to work, it's crucial that you understand that you're not alone.

I challenged you at the beginning of this book to transform yourself. We're in this together, and when you read on, you'll learn a lot that will help you understand what's happening to your body. You'll learn what overweight and obesity mean, whether you are overweight, how big a problem this is in our society, how we got to this point, and finally the dangers of being overweight. You'll also learn how the media influences our perception of healthy and beautiful as well as our perception of how we look, or our body image. When you have all the facts about what it means to be overweight or obese and realize that you're not alone, you'll experience a sense of hope. You'll realize that you can conquer this problem. You'll have a community of peers who understand you, appreciate you, and will encourage you to reach your goals. You'll feel empowered by your new knowledge and new family to achieve anything you set your mind to. You will feel in control. You'll feel strong and powerful. We'll get there together.

Does this sound exciting? Well, keep reading because it's only going to get better!

An Expanding Problem

Dr. William Dietz, the director for the Centers for Disease Control and Prevention's (CDC) Division of Nutrition and Physical Activity, says that the increase in the number of overweight kids is "the most significant nutritional problem in the United States today." Think about that. With all the news coverage of poverty, hunger, anorexia, and adult obesity, the biggest nutritional problem is that *more and more kids and teens are becoming fat.*

And the main reason why we need to focus on fat kids is that they grow up into fat adults. I know it's hard to believe now, but you will be your parents' age someday. And when you get there, you can either be fat, unhealthy, and unhappy, like you are now, or you can change your habits and lifestyle to create a different kind of life for yourself. That's why I wrote this book, to teach you that you don't have to be stuck in this body for the rest of your life. You have the power to change that.

So how bad is the problem? The numbers will shock you. Way back in 1980, before you were born, only 6 percent of kids between the ages of six and eighteen were overweight or obese. Today, as we stated earlier, more than 9 million kids weigh more than doctors think is healthy. And the National Institutes of Health (NIH) contends that the problem is only going to get worse. Experts estimate that 70 percent of overweight kids will become overweight adults. That's nearly three out of four kids! John Foreyt, director of Behavioral Medicine Research Center at Baylor College of Medicine in Houston, Texas, tells us, "This may be the first generation of children who will die before their parents."

Clearly, the number of overweight kids and teens has skyrocketed since the 1970s. But what do "overweight" and "obese" actually mean? How do you know if you're overweight and need to diet? Keep reading—I'll tell you all you need to know.

What Is Overweight?

It sounds obvious, but many teens aren't sure exactly what overweight means. For example, do you know the difference between overweight and obese? Do you know how doctors determine who needs to lose weight and how much they need to lose? Well, in this section, we'll clear up those unanswered questions.

The most basic definition of overweight is *carrying more fat on your body than most people in your age, gender, and height categories.* Obese means *carrying a lot of extra fat on your body, usually more than thirty pounds over your ideal weight.* How is this measured? Doctors use several methods to determine whether a person is at a healthy weight. The method most commonly used is called the body mass index (BMI). BMI is a formula that determines how much body fat you have based on the ratio of your height to your weight. The BMI formula uses your height and weight to calculate a BMI number. That number is then plotted on a chart to see how you compare to other people who are your same age, gender, and height.

Charting BMI for kids and teens is complicated, because body fat percentage and height change so dramatically as they grow. See your doctor to determine whether your BMI is within a healthy range.

How Did We Get So Fat?

There is a lot of controversy surrounding the issue of how 60 percent of adults and 20 percent of kids became overweight or obese. The simple answer is that we're just eating too many calories and eating most of them late in the day. Your body takes in calories in the form of food, burns the calories it needs for fuel, and stores excess calories as fat to burn when it needs it. If you burn the same number of calories as you consume, your weight will stay the same. If you eat more calories than you burn, you will gain weight. If you burn more calories than you consume, you will lose weight. Weight equals calories in minus calories out. You'd think that with such a simple formula, we'd have no problem manipulating the science to achieve our ideal body. But, as I'm sure you know, it's not as easy as it seems.

Fat Genes

You may have heard people claim that being fat runs in their families and say that they have "fat genes." And I don't mean the jeans that you wear! It's true that genes play a role in whether you are fat or skinny. To understand what role genes play in determining

your body type, we need to go back millions of years to our earli-
est ancestors.

Your body actually evolved to hold on to fat. Now we think,
"Why would we ever want to hold on to fat?" Well, our society has
a lot of food that's convenient, high in calories, and readily available. Life wasn't always like that. Our ancestors lived a "feast or
famine" existence. That means that when rain was plentiful and
hunting was good, our ancient ancestors fed on meat, berries,
nuts, and other foods. At other times, when rain was scarce, they
went days or weeks without food. To survive, the body developed
the ability to turn down the metabolism and conserve fat. This
ensured survival by holding on to body fat as an insurance policy.
During these times, the ability to hold on to excess calories as fat
meant that you were more likely to survive famine than someone
who quickly burned off fat stores.

Fortunately, we no longer live a feast or famine lifestyle, but
unfortunately our bodies haven't caught up. We still hold on to
excess fat in case we need it later. So if you have the kind of body
that clings to its extra calories, you probably have a predisposition
to gaining weight. But genes are only part of the story—and a *small*
part at that.

Lifestyle Is the Key

Lifestyle is a much stronger predictor than genes of whether
people will be fat or slim. What is the key to the right lifestyle?
Timing. Most of us have never heard how critical it is for us to eat
the right foods, *at the right times*. The timing of your meals will
determine your blood-sugar levels, and this will determine your
appetite. Remember, when you control your appetite, you control
your weight. Chapter 3 will help you break your old lifestyle habits
like surfing the Internet, playing video games, and watching TV for
too long, or forgetting to eat for hours. The secrets in chapter 3 will
help you think differently. For example, when was the last time

you had a snack at school 3 hours after breakfast? Or even better, when was the last time you had breakfast? Or maybe you feel scared to eat in front of other kids, so you skip lunch. Too many of the teens I have worked with skip too many meals. They're starving when they get home from school, so they overeat.

Mac Attack

In addition to the lack of good meal timing, many teens consume unhealthy foods in too-large portions. The USDA Food Guide Pyramid recommends that everyone eat a wide variety of foods every day, including whole-grain carbohydrates (like brown rice), lots of fruits and vegetables, and lean protein. It also recommends that you limit your consumption of fats, sugars, and refined carbohydrates (like white bread). (We'll go into more detail about nutrition later on.) Most people don't follow these guidelines, however, and instead eat too much sugary cereal, fast food (which is loaded with fat and calories), and drink too many sweetened soft drinks and juice drinks. People are eating these fattening foods in enormous quantities as well. For example, a Quarter Pounder with Cheese, medium fries, and a large Coke at McDonald's adds up to a whopping 1,200 calories! That's over 80 percent of your total daily calories on the 3-Hour Diet™! Chapter 3 will also help you learn how much to eat without counting a single calorie. No kidding!

Keep in mind, however, that the kind of lifestyle your parents create in your home greatly influences your diet and exercise habits. It might be important for your parents to also read this book, if possible. Give them the "Letter to Parents" tear-out sheet in the back right now. Habits are hard to break, which is why losing weight is so difficult for most people. That's why it is so crucial that you start implementing 3-Hour Diet™ principles *now*. You can see how easy it is to get stuck in dangerous and unhealthy patterns.

You can break this pattern, though, and maybe even get your family involved in your journey to wellness.

Media and Advertising

There is another influence on you that may be even more powerful than your lifestyle. I'm talking about the *media*. On average, teens watch three to four hours of TV every day. During that time, you are overwhelmed with ads for foods that are high in calories, sugar, salt, and fat, and low in nutritional value. In fact, one study found that kids watch 10,000 commercials for food, most of it junk and fast food, every year! According to the Institute of Medicine, "There is strong evidence that exposure to television advertising is associated with obesity."

In addition to images of yummy foods, advertisers use beautiful, super-skinny models to showcase their products. The message is supposed to be that you will look like this person or have as many friends as they do if you buy a particular item. And it works—everyone wants to be attractive and admired. But these images are unrealistic and destructive.

Female celebrities are about 23 percent thinner than the average female. It's really difficult to feel good about yourself when images of emaciated teen models look down at you from every billboard. It's not surprising that these images negatively influence body image for both boys and girls. In fact, one study found that 78 percent of teen girls are unhappy with their bodies. This dissatisfaction sometimes results in girls taking drastic measures to achieve this skinny body ideal. Many try crash diets and fail, which often results in even more weight gain. Sometimes this grows into an obsession and teens develop life-threatening eating disorders such as anorexia and bulimia. I'm not saying that advertising is the only cause for these body image issues. But its influence is an important one that can't be dismissed.

Risks of Being Overweight

As you probably already know, being overweight or obese is a bigger problem than just how you look. You may already experience some of the health problems associated with carrying extra weight, such as asthma or other breathing problems, aching joints, and constant fatigue. And as you get older, you'll be at risk for a lot of other serious health problems that used to only happen to people much later in life.

One of the most dangerous risks associated with obesity is developing type 2 diabetes. Diabetes is a disease that prevents the body from regulating its blood-sugar level properly. The disease manifests in two types: type 1 usually occurs in childhood and is not linked to obesity. Type 2, however, is usually associated with severely overweight adults. Ten years ago, type 2 diabetes was almost unheard of in children and adolescents. In fact, it used to be known as adult-onset diabetes. Unfortunately, nearly half of new cases of pediatric diabetes are type 2. The consequences of diabetes are slow-acting but devastating. Type 2 diabetes can result in nerve damage, kidney failure, heart disease, stroke, and blindness. In fact, diabetes is the leading cause of blindness and kidney failure.

Diabetes isn't the only health problem you need to be concerned about. Obesity can also cause hypertension (high blood pressure), cardiovascular disease, stroke, gallbladder disease, fatty liver disease, arthritis, sleep apnea, and other respiratory problems, as well as some cancers such as breast, colon, and endometrial.

These diseases are scary, but you have the power now to reverse the existing damage to your body and turn your life around. Because you're young, you have the time and the ability to prevent these problems from taking strong hold of your body. But you need to implement these changes *now*. The sooner you start living a healthy life, the sooner you can reverse these physical problems and start feeling better. When you start living the 3-Hour Diet™, you'll immediately feel a difference in your weight, health, and emotional well-being.

Remember, you're not alone on this journey. Millions of other teenagers are experiencing the same problems you are. Creating a community of peers is crucial for you to succeed on this plan. Get together with people who will support you, encourage you, and help you achieve your goals. When you realize that you aren't alone, you'll feel a renewed sense of hope and feel empowered to create a different life for yourself. You will be in control.

Let's talk about how the 3-Hour Diet™ works.

PART II
HOW IT WORKS

3-HOUR TIMING

As I stated in chapter 1, the biggest mistake you can make when you're trying to lose weight is to skip meals, because your blood sugar will drop and you'll lose control of your appetite. When you lose control of your appetite, you overeat and gain weight.

But when you eat every three hours—the right foods and the right amounts—you literally change your body's biochemistry and immediately gain *control* over your appetite. That is one of the most powerful benefits of my diet. You will gain control over your eating and the weight will quickly come off and stay off. As a result, you'll feel much more comfortable with your body and be able to wear the stylish clothes you see in magazines, play sports and go to the beach with your friends, and feel more confident than you ever could have imagined. So keep reading, because the 3-Hour Diet™ will change your life forever. For a really motivational story, read about my client Ronika, who was featured on the *Tyra Banks Show*.

RONIKA VAUGHN

POUNDS LOST
40

HEIGHT: 5' 3"

AGE: 22 (was an overweight teenager)

ABOUT RONIKA: Kentucky native

"Before using the 3-Hour Diet™, I was a teenager who was very unhappy with her body and had very low self-esteem. My energy level had decreased to a point where I had become totally inactive. I was suffering physically and emotionally by being over-weight. I knew I had to get in charge of my health, so I chose to do the 3-Hour Diet™.

"As soon as I started the plan, I saw immediate results. Since using the 3-Hour Diet™, I have gone from 155 to 115; I lost 40 pounds and changed my life entirely. My self-confidence grew day after day, and before I knew it I had achieved my goal weight.

"By reaching my goal, I have had many opportunities with beauty pageants and modeling. After I lost the weight, I started entering swimsuit contests and won several beauty contests.

"In the near future, I hope to further my modeling/acting career. I plan to stay on the 3-Hour Diet™ for the rest of my life to stay fit and healthy. If I ever get lucky enough to get a modeling contract, it will be a direct result of the 3-Hour Diet™; it has changed my life dramatically."

continued

RONIKA'S SECRETS TO SUCCESS

▶ Always write grocery lists when shopping. I like to organize mine by different food groups to make sure that I shop efficiently.

▶ When you're cooking, lay out everything you need before you start—pots, pans, protein, veggies, knives, etc. That way you don't waste time looking for what you need in the middle of preparing a meal.

▶ With a Crock-Pot™ and George Foreman® Grill, you'll be able to make tasty food quickly and healthfully!

A Revolution in Eating

The 3-Hour Diet™ really is a revolution in eating. It reveals the secret that so many diets ignored in the past: *When* you eat is just as important as *what* you eat. The 3-Hour Diet™ is what I call Time Based Nutrition. When you eat the right foods at the right times, you will see fat vanish from your body every week and not come back. When you eat at the wrong times, you slow down your metabolism and gain weight.

So why is eating every 3 hours crucial to managing your weight? How does it work? Bear with me as I share the reasons why this diet will keep you slim. We'll embark on a mini science lesson, but trust me, this stuff will absolutely change your life.

Naturally Suppresses Appetite

You'd think that a diet that tells you to eat every 3 hours would cause you to eat more throughout the day instead of less. Well, in fact, the opposite is true.

Remember in chapter 1 when I talked about blood sugar? That's the key. When you eat regularly throughout the day (that is, every 3 hours), you keep your blood-sugar level on an even keel. Keeping your blood-sugar level stable *automatically* suppresses your appetite. Several scientific research studies found that people who ate small meals several times a day binge less often and have fewer cravings than people who only eat one or two large meals every day.

Scientists in the Netherlands conducted a study and found that obese girls who ate small frequent meals had higher levels of a hormone called leptin than obese girls who ate fewer larger meals. Leptin is a hormone produced by fat cells that tells your brain when you're full and it's time to stop eating. The bottom line this study found was that women who ate more frequently felt less hungry and had fewer cravings throughout the day than women who ate sporadically.

Turns Off the Starvation Protection Mechanism

In addition to helping control your appetite, eating every 3 hours will also protect your metabolism. You see, your lean muscle tissue is your metabolism—the more muscle tissue you have, the more calories you burn, even when you're not exercising. It's important, therefore, to not only build new muscle tissue, but also preserve the muscle you already have.

So what does that have to do with eating every 3 hours? When you skip meals, you turn on the starvation protection mechanism (SPM). What is the SPM? It's the body's natural defense against starvation. When you go more than 3 hours without eating, the SPM is triggered and your body preserves fat and consumes precious fat-burning lean muscle. But when the SPM is off, the body burns fat and preserves muscle.

Remember the "feast or famine" concept that we discussed in chapter 2? When conditions were favorable, our ancestors had plenty to eat. But when conditions were bad, they often went days or weeks without eating. That applies to the SPM as well. If you go too long without eating, your body thinks it's starving, so it conserves fat and burns muscle. That's why it's so crucial to eat every 3 hours and keep the SPM turned off.

Many studies support the 3-Hour Diet™ concept of eating every 3 hours to lose fat. Here is a small sample of what research has found:

■ A study published in the *International Journal of Obesity and Related Metabolic Disorders* found that girls who ate small frequent meals expended more energy—burned more calories—digesting their food than did girls who ate large sporadic meals.

■ Researchers in Scandinavia tested two diets on a group of athletes who were trying to lose weight. Although all of them lost the same amount of weight, the participants who ate fewer meals lost mostly lean muscle tissue, while the ones who ate more frequent meals lost almost all fat tissue.

■ One of my favorite clinical trials was reported in the *Journal of Human Clinical Nutrition*: weight loss increased and the loss of lean muscle was minimized in a group of obese women who ate every 3 hours versus another group of obese women who ate every 6 hours.

Increases Basal Metabolic Rate

When you eat a large meal, your body absorbs the nutrients and burns the calories it needs and then stores the excess as fat. Stored fat equals weight gain. However, if you spread that same number of calories out throughout the day, your body receives calories as it needs them. Your cells then take up blood sugar as it becomes available and burns it for energy. As a result, you don't store excess calories as fat and don't gain weight.

Increases Energy Level

Do you often feel tired and sluggish in the afternoon? I remember coming home from school so exhausted that I would collapse on the couch and watch TV until dinner. It was hard to concentrate on homework, and all I wanted to do was take a nap. That slump results from going too long without food. When you let too much time pass between meals, your blood-sugar level drops and your energy plummets. Remember, when you eat every 3 hours, you keep your blood-sugar level stable and provide a continuous supply of energy to your brain and muscles.

Reduces Belly-Bulging Hormone Cortisol

Stress isn't good for you for many reasons: insomnia, headaches, compromised immune system, inability to focus, and lots more. But worst of all, stress can cause your body to release a hormone called cortisol. Low levels of cortisol are important, because a little bit of it regulates blood sugar, blood pressure, and helps with immune function. However, when you're stressed out, you can secrete too much cortisol. High levels of this hormone are associated with increased belly fat.

Luckily, eating every 3 hours actually helps reduce the level of cortisol your body releases. A two-week study conducted by the Department of Nutritional Sciences in Toronto, Canada, found that participants who ate frequent small meals, as opposed to three large meals that contained the same number of total calories, reduced their cortisol levels by more than 17 percent. If these participants could be so successful in only two weeks, imagine how a lifetime of 3-hour eating could benefit you!

Basic Rules for the 3-Hour Diet™

Now you know that this diet is scientifically proven to help you lose weight and keep it off. But how do you make it work for you? You're busy with school, homework, maybe some after-school activities, and hanging out with your friends. How do you add a diet plan to this busy schedule? It's easier than you think. All you have to do is remember three simple rules:

1. Eat your first meal within one hour of waking up in the morning (before school).

2. Eat every three hours (snack and lunch at school).

3. Stay flexible (don't freak if you eat a few minutes late).

That's it! And you won't have to worry about counting calories; I've done that for you, so you never have to wonder if you're eating too much or not enough. It couldn't be simpler. Let's take a closer look at these three easy-to-follow rules.

Eat Within One Hour of Waking Up

You need to eat your first meal within one hour of getting up in the morning. Why? Because your body doesn't get any food as you sleep and consequently turns down your metabolism. That's why it's important to eat and kick-start your metabolism into high gear as soon as possible. If you don't eat within one hour of rising, your body will protect body fat—that calorie-rich tissue you need to survive famine—and consume precious fat-burning lean muscle. If you skip breakfast, you just end up sabotaging your dieting efforts.

Eat Every Three Hours

Eating every 3 hours is crucial to your success on the 3-Hour Diet™. As I explained earlier, eating every 3 hours stabilizes your blood sugar. When your blood sugar is stable, your appetite remains under control so you don't overeat at vulnerable times, like in the evening.

I suggest that you start out with breakfast every day at 7 a.m., or a little before, have a snack at 10 a.m. (at school), eat lunch at

1 p.m., have another snack at 4 p.m., and eat dinner at 7 p.m. Read chapter 6 for tips on eating at school. You can finish your day with a treat, either with dinner or anytime within the next three hours before bed. This is an ideal eating schedule, and I strongly recommend that you follow this pattern.

Stay Flexible

Most teenagers follow unique schedules that may not easily accommodate this eating pattern. No worries! The 3-Hour Diet™ is designed to bend to unique schedules and ensure stress-free dieting by allowing you to move meals and snacks around. Here are a couple of sample plans to show you how you can customize your 3-Hour Diet™ to your schedule.

Typical School Schedule	For the Early Bird
6 a.m.: Breakfast	4 a.m.: Breakfast
9 a.m.: Snack (see chapter 6 for tricks)	7 a.m.: Snack
12 noon: Lunch	10 a.m.: Lunch
3 p.m.: Snack	1 p.m.: Snack
6 p.m.: Dinner	4 p.m.: Dinner
9 p.m.: Treat	7 p.m.: Treat

For the Late Riser	For the Very Late Riser
10 a.m.: Breakfast	Noon: Lunch
1 p.m.: Lunch	3 p.m.: Snack
4 p.m.: Snack	6 p.m.: Late lunch (early dinner) and snack
7 p.m.: Dinner	9 p.m.: Dinner and treat
9 p.m.: Treat and snack	

Although it's important to stay on schedule with your 3-hour eating, real-world obstacles sometimes get in the way. The solution? Stay flexible. As long as you keep close to the 3-hour window, you'll be fine. Ideally, don't allow more than an extra thirty minutes to pass before your next meal or snack.

So now you know how the 3-Hour Diet™ works and how it can help you stay in control of your weight and your health. Remember, skipping meals is the worst thing you can do when you're trying to lose weight. Skipping meals causes your blood sugar to drop, which causes your appetite to spike out of control. As a result, you overeat and gain weight. However, when you feed your body the right foods every 3 hours, you keep your blood sugar, and thus your appetite, under control. You'll eat the right food in the right portions at the right times and not feel hungry or deprived.

With that in mind, fill out and sign the success contract on the following page. Place it on your refrigerator or pantry to remind yourself of your commitment. Every time you start looking for food when you're not really hungry, you'll see your contract and be reminded of your goal and future body. It really helps!

I challenge you to live the 3-Hour Diet™ and see how you can achieve the body and life of your dreams!

THE 3-HOUR DIET™

Filling out this contract will help keep you accountable to your goals. Make three copies and give them to three trusted friends who will support and motivate you in your journey to success.

MY 3-HOUR DIET™ SUCCESS CONTRACT

NAME: _____

TODAY'S DATE: _____

I am going to weigh
this many pounds:

By this date:

SIGNATURE _____

Photocopy this contract and place it on your refrigerator. Join 3HourDiet.com for support and to stay accountable.

THE 3-HOUR PLATE™

So now what do you eat every 3 hours? I've got great news for you. You will lose more weight by eating the **foods you love** than by depriving yourself of your favorite meals. Get ready to break through the conventional approach to dieting—banning foods that actually taste good—and start loving food again!

On the 3-Hour Diet™, there are no banned foods, no counting calories, no restrictions, and no deprivation. You see, when you deprive yourself of your favorite foods, what happens? You start craving those very foods that you told yourself were off-limits! Eventually, your willpower weakens and you binge, sabotaging your success. That's why I've created a plan that allows you to tailor your meals according to the foods you like. Yes, real food, not diet food! If your diet consists of food you find irresistible, it won't be hard to stick to it, right? Moreover, you'll enjoy this irresistible nutrition every 3 hours, so you'll never feel hungry and you'll never be tempted to binge. Your cravings will be under control, your appetite will be under control, and as a result, your weight will be under control.

Knowing that you can eat anything you want on the 3-Hour Diet™ opens a whole world of possibility to you. But it's important to know what foods will accelerate your weight loss, and how to control your portion size to make sure that you aren't eating too much food. This chapter will explain what you need to know about nutrition to help you make healthy food choices. I'll tell you what a calorie is and what it has to do with managing your weight. And I'll introduce you to my 3-Hour Plate™, which gives you a visual idea of how much you should be eating. This is a great tool for eating at school or restaurants. Later on, you'll find recipes and fast food and vending machine guides that make knowing what to eat even easier.

When you start living the 3-Hour Diet™, you'll be amazed at the freedom you have to eat what you like and still lose weight. You'll develop control over your appetite, your cravings, and your weight. You'll feel more powerful and confident than you ever have before.

Open your mind to the possibility that dieting doesn't have to mean deprivation, banned foods, and counting calories. On the 3-Hour Diet™, losing weight is stress-free, effortless, and sustainable for the rest of your life. If you want a quick peek right now, check out the 14-day planner I made for you in chapter 8. Otherwise, keep reading.

What's on the Menu?

My goal with this chapter is to show you a way to eat satisfying, enjoyable meals in healthy quantities that fulfill your body's nutritional requirements and keep your weight under control. Remember, on this plan you'll enjoy three meals, two snacks, and one delicious dessert every day. Those meals will be made up of a balance of the three macronutrients: carbohydrates, protein, and fat. ("Macronutrient" is just a general term to mean a group of nutrients that provide the majority of energy your body needs.) Carbohydrates are your body's main source of fuel; protein is crucial to muscle growth, and tissue repair, and to healthy skin, hair, and nails; and fats make food taste good, make you feel full, and help your body absorb vitamins and minerals. In addition to the macronutrients, you'll consume vitamins and minerals in the form of fruits and veggies to help you fight off disease and keep your vital organs working. All the meals you eat on the 3-Hour Diet™ carefully balance these important food groups so that you lose weight *and* stay healthy. Each of these food groups is crucial to your success.

What Is a Calorie?

We'll keep this simple. In its most basic terms, a calorie is a way to measure energy. Specifically, it's the amount of energy needed to raise the temperature of 1 gram of water 1 degree Celsius. What does that mean for food? Scientists measure the calories in food using a special machine called a calorimeter. They place a food item in the machine and surround it with water before burning it. The heat released by the burning food heats up the water. How hot the water gets tells you how many calories are in the food. If the water goes up 50 degrees Celsius, the food has 50 calories. Cool, huh?

The macronutrients have standard amounts of calories. Carbs and protein have the same number of calories: 4 per gram. Fat, however, has more: 9 calories per gram. That's why a huge plate of vegetables has fewer calories than a small bowl of ice cream—fat simply has more calories. Let's take a look at each of the macronutrients more carefully.

The Lowdown on Carbs

There's a lot of talk lately about carbs; they're the latest enemy in the war against body fat. Low-carb diets—such as Atkins, South Beach, and the Zone—are everywhere, and people are saying no to pasta and yes to steak. But what's the real deal with carbs?

Carbohydrates are basically chains of sugar molecules from plants that come in the form of starch and fiber. Carbs come from grains (like wheat and rice), sugar cane, fruits, and vegetables. Your body breaks down most carbohydrate chains into single simple sugar molecules called glucose, which you use for energy. Carbohydrates are your body's most efficient source of energy. In fact, carbs provide about 40 to 50 percent of your body's energy needs when you're not moving around. Carbs are much easier for your body to break down for energy than protein and fat, so they're kind of your body's go-to source for fuel.

Fiber is different from most carbs, though; it's made up of material that the body can't digest. So instead of being absorbed, fiber travels through the body relatively intact. Fiber is essential because it helps you feel full faster and longer, so you don't eat as much throughout the day. Fiber also helps keep your digestive system functioning smoothly; that's why you may have heard of fiber being called "nature's broom." It keeps food moving through your intestines so that you don't get constipated. Gross, I know, but it's important to stay regular!

Carbs are divided into two categories: whole and refined. Whole carbs are the best. Whole means that the food hasn't gone through a lot of processing—for example, fruits, vegetables, and whole grains. In their whole state, grains are covered by a protective outer layer called the bran that contains most of the grain's fiber. They also have an embryo-like part called the germ, which contains all of their vitamins, minerals, and a little bit of healthy fat. Whole grains are good for you because your body digests them slowly, meaning that you get full faster, stay full longer, and digest the sugar slowly. In other words, whole carbs are kind of a time-released sugar—your blood sugar remains stable instead of fluctuating all over the place. As a result, when you eat whole carbs, you keep your appetite under control, and your body uses fat as its primary fuel instead of muscle. You can find whole carbs in whole grains like oatmeal, brown rice, whole-wheat flour, high-fiber breakfast cereal, quinoa, and 100 percent whole-grain bread.

Refined carbs aren't as good for you as whole carbs. Refined carbohydrates include white flour, granulated sugar, fruit juice, white rice, and white bread. Refined grains have had the bran and germ stripped from them to make them softer, easier to cook, and longer lasting on grocery shelves. However, this process takes away the fiber and vitamins, leaving only starch behind, which your body converts to sugar almost immediately. Your blood sugar spikes, causing a "sugar high," and later plummets, making you feel tired and sluggish.

You need to include carbs in your diet because, like I stated above, they're your body's main source of fuel. Carbs provide the fuel your body needs to keep your lean muscle healthy. When you don't eat enough carbs, your muscles shrivel up, your energy plummets, and you move less. What happens? Your body starts consuming its own muscle for energy, you burn fewer calories, and start gaining fat.

You can eat any kind of carbs you want on the 3-Hour Diet™, but remember that you'll get more bang for your buck if you choose whole carbs instead of refined carbs. To get more whole carbs in your diet, replace orange juice with a whole orange and sugary breakfast cereal with high-fiber whole-grain cereal, and eat your sandwiches on dark whole-grain bread instead of white bread. Try to find a whole carb that you like so that you can incorporate it into your 3-hour eating plan every day.

Power to the Protein

Protein makes up the building blocks for all the cells in your body. It makes up over 50 percent of body tissue. Protein is a major component of your skin, hair, nails, muscles, bone, and blood cells. Protein is made up of chains of molecules called amino acids, some of which the body produces itself and some that you have to get from the food you eat. The bottom line, though, is that protein is critical to weight loss success.

Your body uses protein to create, repair, and maintain all of the tissues in your body, including skin, brain, genetic material, bone, and muscle. Protein is crucial to your muscles; you use it to generate new tissue, repair damaged cells, and prevent the loss of precious fat-burning lean muscle. If you don't eat enough protein, your cells take protein from your lean muscle tissue and recycle it to repair other tissue in the body. As a result, you lose lean muscle mass and your metabolism goes down. You can't store protein for later use, so you need to replenish your protein stores every day with the food you eat.

Protein is also an important factor in keeping your immune system in top shape. Since protein forms the building blocks of your cells, you need to consume enough to give your cells material to work with. If you don't eat enough protein, your body doesn't function as well as it should, and you're unable to rebuild cells when you need them. When you don't have enough protein, your body doesn't have the raw materials it needs to repair your organs, muscles, and other tissues. As a result, you can't fight off infections very well and you get sick. Eat enough protein and you won't catch cold as often!

But protein can be too much of a good thing. You see, converting protein from food into amino acids that your body can use is stressful on your kidneys and liver. Proteins have nitrogen in them, which is converted to ammonia in the liver. That ammonia leaves the body as urine, but the more of it there is, the more toxic it is

to the body. Plus, too much protein can prevent your body from absorbing important vitamins and minerals, which can weaken your immune system as well. Moreover, digesting protein uses up a lot of calcium in your body, calcium that your bones can use to grow stronger. Over the long term, too much protein can result in weak bones and even osteoporosis.

Clearly, protein is essential to weight loss, but some choices are better than others. Try to eat as much lean protein as you can, like skinless white-meat poultry; fish; egg whites; low-fat dairy, like 1% milk and low-fat yogurt; and lean cuts of pork, like loin and tenderloin. You can eat higher-fat proteins, like red meat, on the 3-Hour Diet™, but try to limit your choices to lean cuts, like sirloin and tenderloin.

Figuring Out Fat

As I stated earlier, fats have 9 calories per gram—more than twice the number of calories in a gram of protein or carbohydrate. That's why fat seems so scary to people who want to lose weight. But fat is essential to a healthy diet. The trick is to eat the right fats in the right amounts.

Fats are made up of chains of fatty acids, some of which, like amino acids, are considered essential because they cannot be manufactured inside the human body. Fats are found in all substances, including animal products, plants, fruits, and nuts. Fat serves as a storage system for excess calories and energy to use when food is scarce. Fat helps cells and organs function properly, aids digestion and absorption of vitamins and minerals, and helps keep the body insulated against cold. You've definitely seen fat on cuts of meat and chicken, and fat is also found in dairy products, nuts, avocados, seeds, olives, and coconuts.

Not all fats are created equal, however. There are several different types of fats: saturated, trans (or hydrogenated) fats, and unsaturated fats. Saturated fats come primarily from animal sources like beef, lard (rendered pork fat), bacon, chicken skin, egg yolks, milk, and cheese. Some plant foods also contain saturated fat, like coconut oil, palm oil, and palm kernel oil. Saturated fats are considered "bad" fats, because they're thought to raise cholesterol levels and clog your arteries. Saturated fats are considered unhealthy, but not nearly as unhealthy as trans fats.

Trans, or hydrogenated, fats are relatively new and are considered by health experts to be the most dangerous kind of fat. Hydrogenation is the process of adding hydrogen molecules to fats like vegetable oils to make them solid at room temperature. The reason manufacturers do this is to make the fat—and the products made with the fat—last longer on store shelves. Margarine and vegetable shortening are examples of trans fats, and they're used in store-bought cookies, cakes, crackers, and other baked goods.

Trans fats are considered particularly bad because of the way they affect your arteries. There are two kinds of cholesterol in your body: low-density lipoproteins (LDL) and high-density lipoproteins (HDL). Doctors consider LDL to be "bad" cholesterol, because it's associated with depositing cholesterol inside the walls of your arteries, making them thicker and harder. HDL, or "good" cholesterol, helps eliminate cholesterol from the walls of your arteries, making blood flow more smoothly and reducing the risk of having a heart attack.

Saturated fats are bad because it's believed that they increase both LDL and HDL cholesterol—not good. Trans fats are even worse than saturated fats, because they raise bad cholesterol and lower good cholesterol. Yikes!

Unsaturated fats are considered much healthier than saturated or trans fats. You can always tell whether you're eating a "good" fat, because saturated and trans fats are solid at room temperature and unsaturated fats are liquid at room temperature. Unsaturated fats are typically found in plant sources like vegetable oils, nuts, and seeds. There are two types of unsaturated fats: monounsaturated fats, which include avocado, canola, peanut, and olive oils;

and polyunsaturated fats, which include sunflower, corn, and soybean oils. Unsaturated fats are considered "good" fats, because they're believed to increase HDL levels and decrease LDL levels.

Finally, we come to the omega fats, which are true *gems* when it comes to weight loss. Omega fats are types of polyunsaturated fats that help maintain lean muscle tissue, suppress your appetite, and help you feel full on less food. Omega fats also have the ability to unlock stored body fat so you can burn it for fuel. Omegas boost your body's immune system so you're a lean, mean fat-burning machine! They do this by improving the health of cell membranes, which increases the amount of oxygen circulating throughout your body. Your muscles use this oxygen to convert stored body fat into energy. Omega fats are the only fats that do this! Finally, omega fats even out the body's ratio of insulin to glucagons. Insulin tells your body to store fat, and glucagons signal the body to burn it. Eating a lot of omega fats turns up glucagons and turns down insulin so you burn fat more easily.

Omega fats are found in flaxseed products, soybeans, olives and olive oil, almonds and other nuts, seeds, avocados, and fatty cold-water fish like salmon and tuna.

You can eat any kind of fat you want on the 3-Hour Diet™ and still lose weight, but try to make the majority of your fat intake the heart-healthy kind. Minimize trans fats as much as possible, and use olive oil and flaxseed oil whenever you can. Your arteries will thank you.

Vegging Out

Your mom is right: You should eat your vegetables. Vegetables are among the healthiest foods you can eat because they're full of vitamins, minerals, and other good-for-you-chemicals, known as phytochemicals. Plus, you can eat almost all the veggies you want because they're low in fat, sugar, and calories and high in fiber! Check out chapter 6 for tips on making veggies yummy!

You know how veggies look so pretty and colorful arranged on supermarket shelves? Well, those colors mean that they're chockful of phytochemicals—naturally occurring chemicals that keep your immune system pumping. One serving of green, yellow, red, or orange vegetables gives you up to 100 different phytochemicals, which help you ward off colds and other sicknesses.

All foods contain water, but veggies, particularly broccoli, cucumbers, sprouts, and lettuce, have an extremely high water content. All this extra water will increase the amount of oxygen circulating in your bloodstream, which will help your muscles convert fat to energy. As a result, your metabolism will skyrocket!

Do you know how when you're starving you can scarf down a huge plate of food without noticing when you actually get full? When you're done, you feel stuffed and bloated, right? Well, veggies help with that because they're hard and crunchy, which means that you have to chew them a lot to get them down. Your brain has enough time between bites to signal to you that you're full. And, since they have a lot of fiber, veggies take a long time to digest, so they keep you feeling full longer. When you eat a lot of veggies, you're less likely to overeat and gain weight.

Fresh and Fruity

Fruits have just as many vitamins, minerals, fiber, and phytochemicals as vegetables. In fact, just one apple has one fifth of your daily requirement for fiber! But fruit has more sugar in it and therefore more calories than veggies. Make sure you include fruit in your diet, but try to eat more vegetables than fruit. Limit fruit to one or two pieces per day, preferably with breakfast or as a snack, and eat veggies with your lunch and dinner. Lemons and limes are an exception to this, and you can use them as freely as you would vegetables.

Water

Too many teens consume too many liquid calories. You know what I'm talking about. How many sodas and fruit juice drinks do you have in a day? Just one 12-ounce soda has about 10 teaspoons of sugar and 150 calories. If you have three sodas a day, that adds up to 30 teaspoons of sugar (that's more than a half cup of sugar!) and 450 calories! That means that you're consuming almost one quarter of your daily calories on a standard 2,000-calorie diet in soda alone. Juice is similar in calorie and sugar content, so it's not much better for weight loss.

Water is a dieter's dream beverage. It's refreshing, filling, and totally calorie-free. Water takes up a lot of space in your belly, so it makes you feel full and satisfied. As a result, you'll eat less food and feel less hungry throughout the day. In addition to filling you up, water also makes you feel more energized. When you don't drink enough, you feel tired and worn out, and that's because your heart has to work hard to pump your thickened blood throughout your body. Your muscles and organs don't get all the nutrients and oxygen they need, so they don't work as well.

Water is crucial to keeping all of your bodily functions operating at top notch. After all, your body is made up of 60 to 70 percent water! Water flushes waste out of your system, so your digestive system functions smoothly; it transports nutrients, so your organs get the vitamins and minerals they need; it regulates body temperature; it keeps your skin moist and radiant; and it even relieves some headaches. Your kidneys need water to filter out toxins and prevent kidney stones, and your brain needs water to keep you focused and alert. Water even helps keep your metabolism up by increasing the amount of oxygen in your blood. That means that water helps you lose weight and keep it off!

Most recommendations say to drink at least eight 8-ounce glasses of water every day, but I like to drink more and you should try to, as well. I always tell my clients to drink at least half of their body weight (in pounds) of water (in ounces) every day. That means that if you weigh 170 pounds, you should drink 85 ounces or about ten and a half 8-ounce glasses of water. That sounds like a lot, but it's really not as hard as it seems. Plus, think about all the extra calories you'll burn walking to the bathroom! Spread your drinking throughout the day so you stay hydrated and your body has time to absorb the water.

Don't rely on feeling thirsty to tell you if you need to drink more water; if you feel thirsty, you're already dehydrated. To see if you're drinking enough water, keep an eye on your urine. It should be light-colored or clear, never dark or strong-smelling. Other signs of dehydration include headache, feeling exhausted, or having trouble concentrating. Sometimes we mistake feeling thirsty for feeling hungry, so next time your stomach is growling try chugging a big glass of water. You may not be as hungry as you thought.

Here are some other ways to make sure that you drink enough water:

- Drink a glass first thing in the morning. Put a water bottle by your alarm clock and chug it as soon as you wake up. You may not need that snooze button anymore!

- Drink a big glass of water right before each meal. Since it takes up room in your stomach, you won't be tempted to eat as much as you would if you were famished.

- Carry a bottle of water with you at all times. Stick one in your backpack, your locker, your bedroom, and even leave some in your parents' cars. The more you drink, the better you'll notice when your body needs some hydration, so keep water with you at all times.

HOW TO MAKE WATER TASTE GREAT

In working with teenagers, I've discovered that a lot of them just don't like the taste of plain water. They've been raised on sugary sodas, fruit juice drinks, and other super-sweet beverages, so they think water is tasteless and boring. As you drink more water, you'll get used to it and start to love not only the flavor but also how great it makes you feel. In the meantime, however, I've put together some ideas to help you improve the taste of water so you'll drink more of it.

1. Most tap water tastes nasty—like chemicals. Bottled water tastes better. Try different varieties to find the water you like. If you find a brand that you really like the taste of, you'll be more likely to drink it.

2. A lot of fancy spas offer water flavored with citrus fruits like lemon, lime, and orange. Make your own spa water by filling a pitcher or water bottle with ice water and dropping in a few thin slices of the fruit of your choice.

3. Various naturally flavored waters have made an appearance on the market, such as Propel® Fitness Water by the folks who make Gatorade. These beverages are delicious, all-natural, low-calorie, and convenient. Propel® Fitness Water comes in lots of yummy flavors like melon, peach, grape, lemon, berry, black cherry, kiwi strawberry, mixed berry, mango, and mandarin orange.

The Right Number of Calories for Your Body

On the 3-Hour Diet™, you will consume roughly 1,450 calories per day. Although I've done all the calorie counting for you, I thought you'd like to see how these calories break down into meals and snacks.

MEAL 1: Breakfast 400 calories of balanced nutrients

MEAL 2: Snack 100 calories

MEAL 3: Lunch 400 calories of balanced nutrients

MEAL 4: Snack 100 calories

MEAL 5: Dinner 400 calories of balanced nutrients

MEAL 6: Treat 50 calories

NOTE: Depending on your current weight, you may need to adjust this plan to your personal metabolism. Assuming you weigh less than 200 pounds, the above plan will work for you. However, if you weigh more, make the following changes:

• 200 to 249 pounds: double your snack size to 200 calories

• 250 to 299 pounds: triple your snack size to 300 calories

• 300 pounds or more: quadruple your snack size to 400 calories or add another meal

• As your weight drops, move to the next calorie selection to continue losing two pounds per week.

If you weigh less than 150 pounds and are short in stature (under 5'3"), 1,450 calories might be too much food for you. You can solve this simply by cutting your breakfast in half and eating only 200 calories during this meal, for a total intake of 1,250 calories.

The 3-Hour Plate™

It's easy to throw around numbers of calories for meals and snacks, but it's harder to put those figures into real-world breakfast, lunch, and dinner. I'm a visual guy, so I made 3-hour eating

The 3-Hour Plate™

How it works: For breakfast, lunch, and dinner, use a standard 9-inch dinner plate and fill half the plate with vegetables (fruit is recommended for breakfast) the equivalent of three DVD cases. Then mentally divide the other half into two parts and fill the remainder of the plate with carbohydrates the equivalent of a Rubik's Cube®, protein the equivalent of a deck of playing cards, and then also include a teaspoon of fat to help curb your appetite, the equivalent of a water bottle cap. If you're still hungry after finishing the plate, you can add another plate of veggies or fruit, equivalent to three DVD cases. It's that simple!

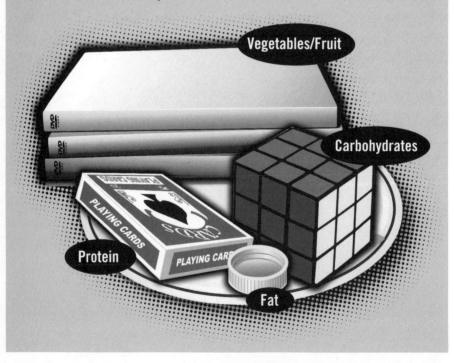

easy for me by creating a visual plate that told me exactly what to eat at every meal. That way, instead of breaking out a food scale or calorie calculator at a restaurant, I could just eyeball my plate and know exactly how much to eat.

The 3-Hour Plate™ holds the three macronutrients—protein, carbohydrates, and fat—as well as essential fruits or vegetables. As I described earlier, each of these food groups performs specific functions in your body and is crucial to weight loss. With my 3-Hour Plate™, you'll be able to enjoy the foods you love as well as a few added foods that will curb your hunger and kick-start your metabolism.

To use the 3-Hour Plate™, mentally divide a standard 9-inch plate in half and fill one half of it with veggies or fruit about the size of three DVD cases. Then divide the empty half of the plate in half again and fill one half with protein the size of a deck of cards, and fill the other half with carbohydrates (like brown rice) the size of a Rubik's Cube®. Then add some fat, the equivalent of a water bottle cap. That's it! Isn't that simple?

For example, you could have two poached eggs, one slice of toast with one teaspoon of butter, and two cups of diced watermelon for breakfast. Then you could have vegetable soup and a sandwich of reduced-calorie bread, turkey, lean bacon, and avocado for lunch, and a taco filled with lean meat plus a mixed green salad for dinner. Doesn't that sound easy?

Remember, timing is everything. Starting with breakfast (yes, you *must* eat breakfast), you need to eat every 3 hours. Remember the rules for the 3-Hour Diet™ in chapter 3?

1. Eat breakfast within one hour of waking up.

2. Eat every three hours.

3. Stay flexible.

Review that section of chapter 3 if you need to, because following those rules is crucial to your success on the 3-Hour Diet™.

Remember that your success also depends on the snacks you eat between meals. Three hours after breakfast and lunch, you should munch on a 100-calorie snack. But if you weigh more than 200 pounds, then make sure to personalize your snacks to your plan (see chart on page 41). Don't forget to eat your snacks, because these small pit stops keep your blood sugar steady, your appetite under control, and your metabolism humming along.

How to Make Your 3-Hour Diet™ Super-Tempting

Now you know all you need to know about the 3-Hour Diet™ and nutrition to succeed with your weight-loss goals. I want you to do a little exercise before we get started, however. This exercise will personalize your 3-Hour Diet™ to your preferences and make it fun for you.

The only way you can have success on a diet is if you enjoy the foods you're eating. You'll only stick with it if you really look forward to your meal times. So right now, think about your favorite foods that fit the 3-Hour Diet™ guidelines. Is it sweet summer peaches or tomatoes, sandwiches, pizza, or crisp apples? Grab a pen and write down what comes to mind in the chart on the next page. Use ideas from the recipes offered in the Resources, starting on page 141. These should be foods that make your mouth water when you think of them. Think about your favorite foods of all time.

Take a look at your food list. Did you ever think that you'd be able to eat those foods and lose weight? Well, I'm here to tell you that you can. The 3-Hour Diet™ is about not banning foods but about learning how to eat the foods you love at the right times and in the right quantities. By not eliminating foods, you'll gain the freedom to enjoy food anywhere, as well as the confidence that comes from knowing that you have the power to control what you eat.

My Ten Favorite Foods

LIST YOUR TEN FAVORITE FOODS HERE:

1. _____

2. _____

3. _____

4. _____

5. _____

6. _____

7. _____

8. _____

9. _____

10. _____

P.S. Photocopy this list and place it on your refrigerator.

BONUS TOOLS

Okay, so how do you accelerate your success? I like to say that there are three Es to losing weight and keeping it off for life: eating, exercise, and emotion. Each one of these factors is crucial, and you won't maximize your results without mastering all three of them. The eating part is obvious; you knew about that when you picked up this book. Exercise is important because, among other things, it increases your lean muscle tissue and helps you burn fat faster than dieting alone. You can lose weight without exercise, but physical activity will help you keep it off for life. Think of exercise as kind of a dieting insurance policy. Mastering your emotions may be the hardest thing you'll have to do. Emotional eating is eating anytime you're not physically hungry; maybe you're depressed, lonely, frustrated, happy and celebrating, or even just bored. That's all emotional eating.

Before we get to the emotional stuff, though, we need to tackle the physical aspects—eating and exercise. You learned all about nutrition and what to eat on the 3-Hour Diet™ in chapter 4. In this chapter we'll talk about how to take your diet to the next level. Some of you might not feel comfortable with exercise yet, and that's okay. You'll get there. I encourage you to start exercising as soon as you feel ready for it, though, because the benefits are amazing. Exercise will tone your muscles and speed up your metabolism so you'll burn calories even when you're at rest (not exercising). Working out also releases feel-good chemicals in your brain that make you feel happier, less depressed, and more confident. Exercise improves your cardiovascular health so that you don't get as out of breath when you're moving around. Finally, exercise will sculpt long, lean beautiful muscles that you'll be proud to show off in tank tops, shorts, or skirts.

I know that you're probably very busy and have school, homework, after-school activities, or jobs that you're responsible for. You're probably thinking, "Jorge, I don't have hours every day to spend in the gym." Well, you don't have to. I've created exercises just for you that only take 8 minutes a day! No kidding! And they don't require you to go to the gym, buy fancy equipment, or even leave the house. You can do these exercises in the privacy of your own bedroom. The 8 Minute Moves® improve your strength and flexibility, increase your lean muscle tissue, increase your metabolism, and help you burn more fat. They'll help you create lean toned arms, flat abs, a high rounded backside, and shapely legs. The 3-Hour Diet™ will help maintain the metabolism you have now, but adding 8 Minute Moves® will take it to the next level. It just doesn't get any easier!

How to Do the 8 Minute Moves®

This chapter shows you two exclusive routines that give you an idea of how powerful the 8 Minute Moves® are. You should do these sessions twice per week, ideally on Tuesdays and Thursdays. This is the minimum amount of exercise you need to do to increase your lean muscle tissue. You can find more exercises like these in my *8 Minutes in the Morning*® books or at www.3HourDiet.com.

Here's the deal: you'll work your upper body on Tuesday and your lower body on Thursday. Each session will consist of two moves; you will do each move for 1 minute (about twelve repetitions) and then switch to the next move. Repeat each move four times. Almost every workout will last 8 minutes. For example, on the day you work your upper body, you will do Knee Push-Ups for 1 minute, followed by the Bird Dog for 1 minute. Then you will do Knee Push-Ups again for 1 minute, and the Bird Dog again for 1 minute. You will continue alternating moves until your 8 minutes are up.

Here's how a typical Tuesday or Thursday morning should go for you:

■ Warm up by jogging in place for 1 minute. The goal is to warm up your joints so that you avoid injury.

■ Perform your 8 Minute Moves®.

■ Cool down with the "Jorge Stretch." Sit on the floor with your left leg straight in front of you. Bend your right leg and put the sole of your right foot against the inside of your left thigh. Your legs will look like the number 4. With your left hand, try to touch either your left ankle or your left toe. This stretch works your left calf, Achilles tendon, hamstring, hip, knee, gluteus, lower-back muscles, shoulder, and wrist. Hold it for 30 seconds and then switch sides.

■ Shower, change, and do whatever you need to do to face the day.

■ Eat breakfast.

It's that easy. And remember, if these exercises become too simple we have a whole library of exercises in my *8 Minutes in the Morning*® books and on www.3HourDiet.com.

TUESDAY | UPPER BODY

CHEST

KNEE PUSH-UP Kneel on a mat on all fours with your knees hip-width apart, your hands slightly wider than shoulder-width apart, and your fingers pointing forward. Bring your pelvis forward so that your body creates a straight line from your knees to your head. Inhale as you lower your chest toward the floor, stopping once your elbows are even with your shoulders. Keep your back straight and your abdominals (stomach muscles) tight the entire time. Exhale as you push back up to the starting position, keeping your elbows slightly bent.

(Note: You can try doing push-ups against the wall if this exercise feels too difficult on the ground.)

BACK

BIRD DOG Kneel on all fours on a mat. As you exhale, lift and extend your left arm and your right leg. Keep your back straight and abs tight throughout the move. When your arm and thigh are parallel to the floor, hold for a count of 3. Inhale as you lower them back to the starting position. Repeat with the opposite arm and leg. Continue to switch sides until you have completed your minute.

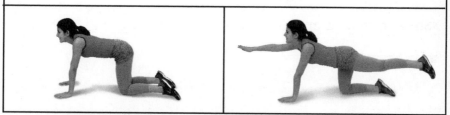

THURSDAY | LOWER BODY

QUADRICEPS

SQUAT PUMP Stand with your feet directly under your hips. Extend your arms in front of you at shoulder height. Check your posture. Make sure your back is long and straight, your shoulders are relaxed away from your ears, and your abdomen is firm. As if you were going to sit back into a chair, inhale as you bend your knees and squat. Bend your knees no more than 90 degrees. (Only squat as deeply as you feel comfortable.) Make sure your knees remain over your ankles (not out past your toes). Keep your abdomen firm and your back straight as you squat. Exhale as you press up to the starting position. Repeat for 1 minute.

HAMSTRINGS

LONG BRIDGE HOLD Lie on your back on an exercise mat or towel on the floor. Rest your arms at your sides and extend your legs, placing your heels against the seat of a chair (not pictured) or against the wall. Bend your knees slightly. Press into your heels as you exhale and lift your hips about 2 inches from the floor. Imagine you are a long bridge, like the Golden Gate Bridge in San Francisco. Hold for up to 60 seconds as you breathe normally.

POWER WALK YOUR WAY TO A HEALTHY HEART

Your 8 Minute Moves® are certainly your most convenient ticket to a faster metabolism and sculpted muscles, but you can do even more to accelerate your success. Some form of aerobic exercise, such as power walking, will not only help you burn off extra calories, but will also condition your heart and lungs, improving your overall health.

I'm a big fan of power walking. Each time you walk briskly for 20 minutes, you burn an additional 150 to 200 calories. If you walk 6 times a week before or after school, you'll burn an additional 1,200 calories. The bottom line is that power walking will help you meet your goal even faster.

I think it's a good idea to buy a pedometer, a handy, inexpensive device sold at many sporting goods stores. Strap it to your waistband or backpack and keep track of how many steps you take in a normal day. Then, every day, try to walk more steps than you did the day before. Eventually, aim for 10,000 steps a day. That's the number doctors and other experts say will get your heart pumping and help you lose weight.

Although 10,000 steps may sound like a lot, you can easily add in more steps with the following tactics:

- Take a brisk 10-minute walk before school. It will help clear your mind and ready you for the day ahead.

- Get some of your friends to walk around the school track with you during lunch. That will be a nice break from sitting all day in class.

- Drink plenty of water (which will boost your metabolism as well). You'll take more trips to the bathroom, increasing your walking time!

- Walk briskly between classes. Even these small bursts of exercise can get your heart rate up.

- Walk with your family in the evening. It will bring you closer.

Overcoming Emotional Eating

Amy was always a chubby kid and had trouble making friends at school. Before she came to see me, Amy thought about food constantly. During her morning classes, she'd daydream about what she'd get from the cafeteria for lunch. In the afternoon, she would try to guess which fast-food joint she and her mom would swing by for dinner. After dinner, she would plop in front of the TV with a bag of chips or a pint of ice cream and munch away. Before she knew it, she would eat the whole container.

When I talked to Amy, I learned that her dad left and her parents divorced when she was thirteen years old. Her mom started working two jobs to support them and had no time to cook healthy meals, and she was away a lot more. Before her parents' divorce, Amy'd been a little chubby, but she had gained about 60 pounds in the two years since her dad left.

Amy was a classic emotional eater. Instead of talking to someone about how sad she was over the breakup of her family and her dad leaving, she looked to food to make herself feel better. To make up for all the food she ate at night, she'd skip breakfast and try not to eat a lot at school. By the time she got home, she'd be starving; she'd eat from dinnertime until she went to bed.

But when Amy started the 3-Hour Diet™, she learned how to stop that vicious cycle of emotional eating. She gained control over food and realized that chips and cookies weren't going to make her feel less sad about her parents' divorce. She learned that only human attention and nurturing could make her feel better.

What Is Emotional Eating?

Does Amy's story sound familiar to you? Have you ever used food to make yourself feel better when you were sad? Have you ever tried to support or comfort yourself with food?

Don't feel bad, because you're not alone. Millions of people eat when they're not hungry, and when they do, it's for emotional reasons. Eating when you're not hungry can indicate a deeper problem, some sort of void that you're trying to fill with food. It's not your stomach that's hungry, it's your heart. Unfortunately, emotional eating is so common that it's the number one saboteur of all diets.

It's no surprise that people turn to food for emotional support. Life is stressful. Like Amy, a lot of my clients come from divorced homes, some of them have been abused, some of them have parents who work a lot or are too busy to give them the love and attention they crave. Food is a crutch for a lot of us, and we think that it will get us through sad or lonely times.

But food doesn't really help us out in times of need, does it? Do we feel any better when that pint of ice cream is gone? No—in fact, we usually feel worse. We're really craving human attention or affection when we think we're craving chocolate chip cookie dough. It tastes good going down, but when you're stuffed with food, you still feel that emotional void that you were trying to fill. It's like trying to fill a hole in the desert with water. Once the water seeps in, you're left with the same hole that was there before. All you've done is gain calories and fat.

The key is to learn to distinguish between nutritional hunger and emotional hunger. Nutritional hunger is your body's need for the calories, vitamins, minerals, and other nutrients it requires to function. On the other hand, emotional hunger is a need for love, acceptance, warmth, companionship, and affection from other people. You need to learn to feed this need with human contact instead of food.

When you overcome emotional eating, you will:

1. *Achieve true, long-lasting freedom.* When you eat emotionally, you don't enjoy food as much as you should. You're eating to relieve pain, so you come to associate food with negative emotions. However, when you stop eating emotionally, you have the

freedom to enjoy a treat once in a while without guilt and without reminding yourself of bad times.

2. *Stop the self-sabotage.* One of the most devastating obstacles to successful weight loss is self-criticism. Emotional eating often leads to binges, which lead to feelings of anger, helplessness, and incompetence. When you control your emotional eating, you feel stronger and more powerful. You'll tell yourself positive things like, "I really wanted another helping of pasta, but I didn't eat it. I have so much willpower now!" You'll encourage yourself to succeed instead of dragging yourself down.

3. *Stop being enslaved by food.* Food is everywhere you go, at school, at the mall, at home. And portions are huge. You might feel walled in behind mounds of candy, cookies, and tortilla chips and think you have to eat your way through. It's just not true. Find friends or family who will break down those walls and give you the love and support you truly crave.

The bottom line is that when you stop eating emotionally, food will become a source of pleasure in your life again—a pleasure you can control. What you need to do is find other methods of coping with sadness, loneliness, depression, anxiety, or boredom that won't widen your waistline. You need to make a new choice and decide not to use food as a crutch. Here's my 3-step plan:

Step 1: Accept Yourself

The first thing you need to do to lose weight is to learn to love yourself. I know it sounds cheesy and sentimental, but bear with me, because this stuff can make the difference between keeping the weight off for life or regaining it all in a year.

You need to learn to love and respect your body. Your body is a miracle worker that does millions of amazing things every day. Take care of it and give it the respect it deserves.

To love your body, you must start to treat yourself as your own best friend. Who else is going to take care of you as well as you take care of yourself? Your parents may take the best care of you they can, but let's face it, who actually controls the food you put in your mouth, the amount of sleep you get, and how much you move your butt every day? You do! As a teenager, you're just starting to become more independent and make some decisions for yourself. Don't you want those decisions to be good, healthy ones that help you get where you want to be? You need to become your own best friend and treat yourself well.

To become your own best friend, you need to do three things:

■ Accept your current self.

■ Get motivated.

■ Use a journal to express your feelings.

Accept Your Current Self

A lot of my clients tell me that they hate their bodies. Hearing this makes me sad, because I know it means that they're not treating their bodies very well. Think about it. How do you treat something you hate? You think and speak badly about it, avoid it, try to ignore it and focus on other things. What's the result? It just gets worse because you're not nurturing and caring for it.

Many people think that they'll start loving their bodies once they reach their goal weight. It just doesn't work that way. In fact, some of the thinnest people I know hate their bodies and can't stand looking in the mirror. Being thinner won't make you accept yourself any more; it's actually the reverse. As soon as you start loving and accepting your body, you'll become more successful at losing weight. Once you start treating yourself well by eating healthfully and exercising, the pounds will melt off. You need to start respecting yourself now, no matter how much weight you have to lose.

Get Motivated

Once you start treating yourself as a treasured friend instead of a hated enemy, you're ready to get yourself motivated. From working with a lot of teens, I've learned that the secret to getting motivated is having a specific goal in mind.

To set your goal, think about what your ideal weight is. Make sure your goal weight is appropriate for your age, height, and body type. It's important that you see a doctor before you begin this or any other diet. I am giving you a way to figure out what your ideal goal weight should be, but you need to talk about it with your doctor and see if he or she agrees. Together, decide how many pounds you have to lose and divide that number by two. That number is approximately how many weeks it will take you to reach your goal. So, if you want to lose 50 pounds, you will reach that goal in about twenty-five weeks; if you want to lose 100 pounds, it will take you about fifty weeks, and so on. Take out a calendar and circle the date when you'll reach your goal.

If you have a lot to lose, your goal date might seem a long way off. In order to keep yourelf motivated, I want you to set mini goals for yourself along the way. When you've lost 10 pounds, for example, maybe treat yourself to a new CD or video game. When you've lost 20 pounds, enjoy a manicure/pedicure with your girlfriends. Whatever works for you. Keep yourself inspired to stay on track.

Another way to ignite your deepest motivation is to visualize yourself at your goal weight. Take a couple of pictures of yourself and paste your favorite in the following chart. Take pictures at all stages of your journey so you'll have a visual reminder of how far you've come.

Seeing pictures of your new figure can inspire you to continue toward your goal even more than seeing the progress you've made. Thanks to technology, you can see a preview of what your future body will look like. This revolutionary photo technology was cre-

Your Current Body and Future Goals

Talk to your doctor to find out an ideal weight that is healthy and realistic for you. Subtract that number from your current weight. That's your weight-loss goal.

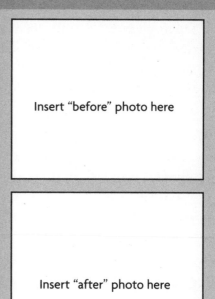

Insert "before" photo here

Insert "after" photo here

Then, to determine a target date for achieving this goal, divide your weight-loss goal by 2. That's the number of weeks it will take to reach your goal. Consult a calendar and find the exact date you will achieve your *happy goal weight*.

Please record your answers to the following:

Current weight: _____

Current thigh circumference in inches: _____

Current hip circumference in inches: _____

Current waist circumference in inches: _____

Happy goal weight: _____

What date will you reach your goal weight: _____

ated by a Canadian company called My Virtual Model, Inc., who has a website that can create a model of your future body. Paste that picture next to your before picture on the chart. These "after" images are extremely powerful motivational tools, because they give you a visual image of what you're working toward. Seeing yourself at your goal weight will help you stay focused on your goal.

One more way to stay motivated is to do visualization exercises. Imagine how your life is going to change when you have a body that you're proud of and you're confident and happy. Think about any day in the future after you've reached your goal weight. Starting from the moment you wake up in the morning, describe what your life is like now. How do you feel when you get up? What do you wear? How do people act toward you?

These exercises might seem silly, but they're really good at pointing you in the right direction and keeping you motivated. It's important to begin any journey with the end in mind, as motivational speaker Stephen Covey has said. To be successful, visualize your goal—a thinner, fitter, more confident you—before you begin.

Use a Journal to Express Your Feelings

It's hard to believe that something as simple as writing down your thoughts and emotions could help you lose weight, but it does. Writing in your journal makes your thoughts and emotions seem more real. It also provides you with a written account of all your hard work, so if you start to lose motivation, you can look back and see what other obstacles you've overcome. You can read about various coping strategies you've used to remind yourself of how to get through hard times. Your journal will serve as a friend who loves you and accepts you unconditionally; it will listen to you without bias or judgment. Plus, research has shown that people who write in journals improve their physical and mental health. Writing in a journal is a very calming and soothing act that improves your total well-being.

To get started, designate a notebook as your weight-loss journal. Take it with you everywhere so you can write in it whenever you feel frustrated, angry, sad, or tempted by food. Make it a habit to write down every feeling you have and how you got through every temptation.

I've included space for you to record your feelings, thoughts, triumphs, and failures in your planner in chapter 8. That's how important it is to me that you start writing down your emotions and experiences.

Step 2: The People Solution™

Like I said earlier, when you eat emotionally, you're substituting fried chicken and potato salad for hugs and kisses. You really want human contact, but you're settling for food. Just think—if you had contacted a buddy for a shoulder to cry on, you might not have cried into your mac 'n' cheese!

Study after study has shown that people need contact with other people from the time we're born. Babies who don't get cuddled and loved develop what's called "avoidant attachment style," which means that they have trouble developing meaningful relationships for the rest of their lives. Some neglected babies may suffer physical problems, become handicapped, or even die. So it's crucial that we connect with other people for attention and affection.

Unfortunately, many of us don't get the kind of love and attention we need, especially from our parents. Maybe, like Amy's parents, they divorced when we were young and Dad moved away. Or maybe they're married, but they're busy working to pay bills, so they're not home very often. That's a big reason why so many of us are overweight. We're trying to fill a void of family love with food.

Not everyone who's overweight has problems at home, but whatever the cause, the solution isn't going to be in a bowl of buttered popcorn. You need people! As soon as you start fulfilling your emotional needs with the comfort and support you really crave, you'll no longer try to fill that hole with food.

I have a perfect, calorie-free solution to provide you with the support you need to be successful. I call it the People Solution™. OK! You've recognized that you're eating emotionally and why, you've accepted your current self, now you're ready to move on to the People Solution™.

Build an Inner Support Team

To get started on the People Solution™, think of a bunch of people whom you can count on to support you on your journey and keep you motivated. I like to call this group of people your Inner Support Team. This group can include your school friends, family, teammates, or youth group members—anyone you feel comfortable opening up to. These people must be willing to listen to you sincerely and respond to you honestly.

Start by thinking of seven people and list them in the space on page 61.

If you can't think of seven people, that's okay, just fill in as many as you can. Invite them to join your inner circle by sending them a nice letter asking for their support. Once they agree to support you, divide them into the following categories:

■ *E-mail buddies:* Pick three of your seven people to be e-mail buddies and write their e-mail addresses in the Contact Info column. If you're feeling an emotion that makes you want to eat when you aren't hungry, write to one of your e-mail buddies and tell them how you feel. For example, you might write, "I just had a huge fight with my mom, and I'm really upset. I feel like she's trying to run my life. All I want to do is raid the fridge." Ask your e-mail buddies to respond within twenty-four hours with encouragement and support.

■ *Phone buddies:* Pick another three people and ask them to be your phone buddies. Fill out their cell phone number in the Contact Info column. These buddies will help you out when you need immediate support. If you find yourself wanting to tear into a bag of Doritos®, call one of your phone buddies. He or she will know exactly what words will help you resist the temptation.

■ *Accountability buddy:* The last person left on your list is your accountability buddy. Arrange a time once per week, preferably at the beginning of the week, to chat with your accountability buddy for about thirty minutes. Share your successes and failures, when you felt weak and when you felt strong. This person should be someone you admire, someone fit and healthy who can encourage and inspire you on this journey. Write your accountability buddy's contact info on the chart.

My Support Team

List the seven people on your support team in the spaces provided.

NAME	TYPE	CONTACT INFO
1.		
2.		
3.		
4.		
5.		
6.		
7.		

Next you will place those seven people into the following buddy groups:
- 3 e-mail buddies
- 3 phone buddies
- 1 accountability buddy

Expand Your Inner Support Team

Now that you've picked your inner support team, you're ready to expand your safety net by adding more people. The more support and accountability you have, the more likely you are to stay on track.

There are lots of ways to expand your Inner Support Team. I suggest that you go on the Internet and join our online club at www.3HourDiet.com. Thousands of teens just like you chat with, support, encourage, and listen to one another on our support boards and chat rooms. You'll also have access to other useful tools that will make your weight loss easier.

If you don't have Internet access or prefer face-to-face human contact, you can start a weekly weight-loss group in your hometown. You'll be able to share diet tips and secrets, healthy recipes, or exercise strategies. You might even make some new friends. A bookstore or library is the perfect place to hold these meetings. As a matter of fact, there are already 3-Hour Diet™ meetings taking place across the country.

If you can't find a 3-Hour Diet™ club in your town, talk to the manager of a local bookstore, show him or her this book, and say that you'd like to start a book club. Lots of my teen clients started similar clubs and made a bunch of new friends! And if I'm ever in your hometown, I might just have to stop by one of your meetings!

Step 3: Conquer the Night

Getting through the hours after dinner and before you go to bed without pigging out is one of the hardest parts of sticking to a diet. Why is this time so hard? You've eaten dinner, maybe you're working on some homework or watching TV, listening to music in your room, or playing computer games. There aren't a lot of distractions, and maybe there isn't anyone there to see you eat. You hear the fridge and cupboards calling your name.

It might start out small with a cookie or single scoop of ice cream. But that doesn't fill the void, so the next thing you know, you've eaten the whole box of cookies or pint of ice cream.

The key to controlling these weak moments is the same as it is for any other time of day: support. You're looking to satisfy a craving for human bonding with food, and it'll never work. You need contact with people—loving, warm, affectionate contact to satisfy that need. If you find yourself overeating at night, plan support into your evenings. Give yourself another option to turn to instead of food, and you're more likely to be successful. Try these suggestions:

■ As soon as you finish your dinner and treat, go online. Vent your need for contact, frustration with the day, or school pressures online. Go to www.3HourDiet.com and chat with your buddies, send e-mails to your Inner Support Team, and share your feelings. You'll feel better and stronger; you'll be more able to fight temptation.

■ Write in your journal every evening. When you feel tempted to raid the fridge, take a few minutes to scribble in your journal. Write down things that happened to you, things you said or did, how you felt that day, what made you happy or sad. Get it all out. By the time you're done, you will probably feel more relaxed, in control, and not as drawn to the kitchen.

■ Call or meet a friend every evening. Call or visit someone you can really open up to every night. Maybe this person is your mom, dad, or sibling. Maybe it's your best friend who lives nearby. Chat with them. Make sure that this is someone you can feel comfortable with and truly trust.

Remember, there are three Es that you have to master to lose weight successfully and keep it off: eating, exercise, and emotion. You now have all the tools you need to conquer each one of these components. Hone these skills and you'll achieve freedom to enjoy food again, stop sabotaging your success, and stop being enslaved by food. Use my 3-step plan—accept yourself, use the People Solution™, and conquer the night—and you're on your way to lifelong weight control.

Let's see how other teens just like you made this plan work for them.

REAL TEENS TELL ALL

As the diet and fitness coach for the *Tyra Banks Show*, I got to meet an inspiring group of teenagers who needed some help. These teens were good kids who were mistreated at school, felt uncomfortable eating at restaurants and at school, and felt like people stared at them wherever they went. They desperately wanted to lose weight. Their parents wanted to help them, but they didn't know what to do. These kids needed a role model, someone they could look up to who would show them how to lose weight healthfully and keep it off for life.

I feel very lucky that I was able to be a role model to these kids and help them become fit and healthy. After working with my team and me, these kids learned all about the 3-Hour Diet™ and lost weight! They applied the principles to their lives. They figured out how to make sure they ate breakfast every day and ways to eat at school so they didn't feel like people were judging them. They got their families involved in their efforts and started eating healthier meals at home. They learned valuable tips and tricks that I'm excited to be able to share with you in this chapter.

So come meet these wonderful kids. They will be awesome role models for *you* as you start your journey. It's really great to have someone to look up to, someone who's been where you are and knows what you're going through. These kids will provide you with helpful hints to get you to your goal. Learning their 3-Hour Diet™ tips and tricks will make the diet easier and more fun than you could have imagined. Take advantage of what they have to offer, because these kids know what they're talking about!

Let's meet these incredible teens.

Able was seventeen years old. Able was heavy since he was a baby; he weighed 90 pounds when he was two years old. He experienced a lot of health problems as a result of his weight: He had breathing problems and was hospitalized with bronchitis for about a month, he had problems with depression, and he couldn't move around very easily. Able had never ridden a bike and feared that he wouldn't wake up in the morning. He enjoyed playing video games, reading, listening to music, and creating art. Able told me that he had come to accept that he was fat.

Molly was fifteen years old. She ate food to comfort herself when she was depressed or having a bad day. She dropped out of school to be homeschooled because kids said mean things and threw rocks at her. Molly didn't like to eat at restaurants because people stared at her. She tried a lot of other diets, but she didn't see results quickly enough so she stopped. She enjoyed dancing, listening to music, and hanging out with her friends.

Dakotah was twelve years old. Dakotah and his family loved to celebrate happy occasions with food. He loved steak, ice cream, calamari, second helpings, and cooking big meals. Dakotah's whole family had weight problems. He was called "Fat Albert" at school and sometimes wore a girdle to hide his chest. Dakotah didn't like to exercise, but he loved to play basketball, listen to music, travel, read, and use the computer.

Cassandra was sixteen years old. Cassandra said that she didn't eat a ton of food, but she ate the wrong foods at the wrong times. She ate fast food two to three times a week and liked a lot of fried foods and sweets. She hated vegetables, salads, and salad dressings. She told me that she came across to other people as confident, but she wanted to lose weight to feel better about herself inside. She was looking forward to being able to shop off-the-rack instead of buying her clothes at special plus-size stores.

Those are the awesome kids who will serve as inspiring and helpful role models as you begin your journey to the body of your dreams. The following is a conversation I had with these kids in which we discussed what some of their best strategies were for making the 3-Hour Diet™ work for them. Take notes and use all of their tips—they're great!

JORGE'S INTERVIEW WITH 3-HOUR DIET™ TEENS

Jorge: What's been your number one key to success on the 3-Hour Diet?

Molly: Eating smaller portions and lots of vegetables and fruits instead of french fries and chips.

Dakotah: I think that the biggest secret for me has been that everybody is so supportive. And that's not really a secret, but I think that helps you stick to the diet. But the support system that I have is what really motivates me and what really keeps me focused.

Jorge: Tell us about your support. What's your support system and how did you create it?

Dakotah: My support system is mostly my family, and everybody wants to be on it, everybody wants to help. Everybody is encouraging me to change my life, my mother especially, because she didn't know how deeply I was affected by my weight, and I think that really pushed her to help me even more. And also, when I went on the show I wasn't just seeking help for myself; I really wanted to help other people because I felt like I was alone in my problem. But I really wasn't. There are a lot of other people who have weight problems. I want to let other teens or preteens who are in my predicament know that they're not alone and they can do it. If I can do it, they can do it too.

Jorge: Now, what would you tell kids out there who think they are all by themselves, kids who don't think they have a support system? What can they do to support themselves better?

Dakotah: First, don't feel like you are alone. Because something will happen about your weight. Just put in the effort and it will happen. But if you don't have the support system at home, you can get online and go to Mr. Jorge's website (www.3HourDiet.com) and you can go to the chat room thing and find people to help you. Maybe they don't have the support system either. But, you all can really help each other. You all can balance each other out. Definitely.

Cassandra: I think one of the big things is just being in the mindset of doing the diet. And just doing it for yourself. And not really letting other people get in the way of that. I hang out with friends a lot, and a lot of them try not to eat a lot of the things that they know I'm going to want, that I can't have. But also, like, I think people shouldn't really have to do that and that you should be able to control yourself. You should be able to say no and you know, in your mind, because you're on a diet and you're not going to cheat just to gain a pound.

Jorge: What has been your biggest obstacle so far with the plan?

Molly: The biggest obstacle is if I'm having a bad day I want to binge because I'm depressed or whatever. That's probably been the hardest. I just tell myself that if it's not on one of my 3-hour marks, then I don't need to eat, because it's emotional eating and not healthy eating. And then probably not being able to go to a fast-food place and get a double cheeseburger and french fries. But I can still get something at a fast-food restaurant.

Cassandra: The biggest obstacle, hmm. Probably at first, eating smaller portions of food. Now I guess I'm just used to eating smaller portions. If I eat a little bit too much, it makes my stomach hurt where I'm full.

Able: Probably knowing what to eat.

Jorge: Have your parents been helpful? Did they read the original 3-Hour Diet™ book? And if they did, what have they done to help you out?

Molly: My mom and the rest of my family have been very helpful. She always makes sure that she cooks everything the right way. My whole family volunteered to read the book, so we could all work on it together. Push your family to read this book because it really opens their eyes. It helps with cooking healthy meals.

Cassandra: Well, my mom, of course, supported me from the beginning. She read the book. And she helps me out if I need something, like if I need more food or I need fruit or snacks. She takes me to the store and helps me get what I need or whatever. My dad is the same way. If I tell him I need something, he'll go to the store and get it for me or he'll take me or whatever.

Able: My mom's amazing. She's been doing the diet with me.

Jorge: What are you doing to make vegetables more fun?

Molly: I would just get no-calorie or really low-fat dressing and celery. I got low-fat peanut butter. And fat-free cream cheese.

Dakotah: I like to have broccoli with a tablespoon of cheese sauce over the top of it, just a little bit. But then you just have to limit the other things. Maybe have meat that's just a little bit leaner. But that's definitely a tip for the broccoli. I like mine plain. But whoever may not like theirs that way can put butter on it and a little bit of salt because that always makes it taste good. And you can put the cheese sauce over it.

Jorge: What was that about cheese sauce? That sounds good. So, what did you find?

Dakotah: My mom knows how to make a good cheese sauce. And we just started to limit it down from what we used to eat. We always had vegetables but never as much as we should have before. So my mom makes cheese sauce for me. We always have some sharp Cheddar cheese, but we found one that had a little bit less fat. And we started using that. I get about a tablespoon.

Cassandra: Well, I really still don't eat that many vegetables, but I try now. Just find salad dressing that you like. I like Italian and vinaigrettes.

Jorge: Now, tell us about your liquids. How much water are you drinking?

Molly: I drink nothing but water. I have a half-gallon jug, and I drink about three of those a day. If I don't really want water, then I use Crystal Light.

Dakotah: I love Crystal Light.

Molly: Yeah, you know, no calories or anything in it, so it's like you're drinking a fruit juice or something.

Jorge: And no calories. You see, that's the trick because soda drinks have like 150 calories in one drink and it doesn't fill you up. So you're still hungry. If you guzzle three or four of those, my gosh, that's like a quarter pound of fat you're going to add to your body right away, and just pure sugar.

Jorge: How do you manage school and food?

Dakotah: Actually, I had a problem, and I slipped on that a little bit. I was eating in one of my classes because I got to school a little bit late, and I was having my breakfast so I can stay on the diet. And my teacher said, "Why are you eating in my class?" He embarrassed me in front of the whole class. And I thought to myself, I don't understand when I'm trying to do something to help myself if people are always going to put it down. But, you know, I never really talked to that teacher about it. I didn't want it to be a big thing. So I just stopped eating in that class all together. I would eat in another teacher's class. That teacher heard about me being on the *Tyra Banks Show* and is supportive of it. So I just eat in that class, and then I don't have to eat at school besides lunch.

Jorge: So the trick there, it sounds like, is to find the best teacher to support you and try and eat around their time, right?

Dakotah: Yeah, because, actually, if you can tell your teacher that you're trying to do something to help better yourself, I'm sure any teacher would like to help you with that. But I asked to speak with the other teacher outside, but they said to say whatever it was out loud. I really didn't like that. So I just left it alone and just went on with my day. But you should definitely tell your teachers so that they know why you're eating. You won't look stupid in front of the whole class when she calls you out on it. You just tell her about it. . . .

Cassandra: My snacks usually come in wrappers that make noise in a quiet classroom. So I take little containers and I put all my food in there, so I can just open the container and eat it out of there. That way it doesn't make as much noise.

Jorge: Oh, that's great! That's a great trick!

Dakotah: Yeah, I do that too.

Jorge: Where do you see yourself in the next year?

Molly: I see myself even smaller, hopefully. Healthier. And more confident. More happy and not so depressed as I was before. And I plan on going back to school next year.

Dakotah: In one year I really see myself being well and with a smaller chest, and skinnier. I also see myself as somebody who sets an example for everybody else and lets them know that they can do it just as well as I can. I want to reiterate that I used to feel that I could not do this by myself, I thought I was alone, because nobody understood. But people do understand. And I know I understand. Because I felt like that. If you feel like that, you're not alone. Hopefully I'll see myself as a role model and be able to help other people in any way I can.

Cassandra: I see myself healthier and happier. More comfortable with myself and just better, happier as a person. I want to go shopping at a store where I've never been able to buy clothes before. It would be nice to not worry about whether they have my size.

Able: To lose weight and get a job.

These kids worked really hard on the 3-Hour Diet™ and lost a significant amount of weight. Visit www.3HourDiet.com for updates on their progress. I hope you found something useful in their comments to help you in your 3-Hour Diet™ journey. Remember, to lose weight successfully and keep it off, it really helps if you have a role model. This should be someone who can inspire you and can keep you motivated. Look to these teens, who have already been through your journey, for tips and tricks to make your diet easier and more fun. Try some of their secrets for eating at school, like putting bars with loud wrappers in separate containers. I really like that one! Learn from your role models and your experience will be simpler and more enjoyable than you ever could have imagined.

PART III
THE PROGRAM

BEFORE YOU START

Working with so many teenagers over the years, I've discovered that the first two weeks of your plan are the most critical. In the first fourteen days, you'll develop the momentum that will sustain you all the way until you reach your goal.

One of my first teen clients was a young man named Doug. Doug was eleven years old when I met him through his parents, Lisa and Paul. Doug had struggled with his weight for many years. The other kids in school made fun of him and called him fat. He wasn't too athletic and had a hard time keeping up with everyone else in gym class. He told me that he was *not* happy.

When I asked Doug about what he ate every day, he told me that his mom always kept healthy food in the house, but he just ate too much of it. He sometimes skipped breakfast and didn't eat a lot at school, and by the time he got home, he was just starving. He would come home and eat so much, especially Chinese food, that he sometimes felt like he was going to throw up. He was eating too much food at the wrong times.

The first thing I did was share with Doug the power of eating every 3 hours. I taught him that by eating every 3 hours, he would stabilize his blood sugar, which would get his appetite under control. That way he wouldn't be starving when he got home from school and eat everything in sight.

I created a fourteen-day plan for Doug that showed him how to space his meals throughout the day. Doug had his day organized so that he always knew when he would eat his next meal or snack, and he always knew what he was going to eat. Doug used his planner and started exercising, and before he knew it, he lost all of his excess weight. See page 77 for Doug's full story. I'm so proud of him. He's now thirteen years old, a super athlete, and a true role model for all teens.

The next chapter is a fourteen-day planner like the one I created for Doug. I challenge you to use this planner to get you started on the 3-Hour Diet™. This planner will jump-start your diet and help ensure that you stay motivated and reach your goal.

Here's your game plan:

■ *Visualization.* Each day begins with a visualization. Visualizing what you want your body or life to be like is key to your success. Visualizations will build inner strength as you develop a picture in your mind of your ideal you. What you envision, you create; so create a positive future for yourself and you'll achieve it.

To truly visualize the new you, you must be relaxed and calm. Free your mind of any negative thoughts, resentments about your day, or any other clutter that could get in the way of your positive mental picture. Do whatever you need to do to create a calm, relaxed environment: Play fun or soft music, light a candle—whatever works for you. You can even record these visualizations on your computer or a CD so you can listen to them instead of reading them. If you want more visualizations, pick up my

3-Hour Diet™ CD; I've recorded all of them so you can listen to me read them to you any time (go to www.3HourDiet.com or visit the iTunes store).

■ *Meal Plan.* The meal plan outlines everything that you're going to eat for each day. All you have to do is write in the times of your meals and snacks and check them off as you eat them. Here's a great rule: you can swap out any of these meals! If you don't like Monday's breakfast, swap it out for Wednesday's breakfast or even Friday's lunch if you want. This plan is totally flexible.

Remember that if you weigh over 200 pounds, you increase your snack size; and if you're under 5′ 3″ and weigh under 150, you cut your breakfast in half. Refer back to chapter 3 if you need a refresher on 3-Hour Diet™ guidelines.

■ *Daily Tip.* Each day includes a daily tip to help you incorporate the diet into your life. Read the tips every day and think about how these suggestions might help you reach your goal.

■ *Journal.* Finally, I've included a space for journaling. This is a great opportunity to meet one-on-one with yourself—your own best friend—and reflect on your day. Write down all your thoughts, feelings, successes, and challenges for the day. This is a very calming exercise that will help you stay focused and not overeat in the evening.

So now you have an overview of what your next two weeks will be like. Remember, the first fourteen days are crucial to getting you started and creating the momentum that will keep you going until you reach your goal.

Now you're all ready to get started on your 3-Hour Diet™ plan. I challenge you to start your fourteen-day plan on the next full day! Tomorrow, wake up in the morning, eat breakfast, have your snack 3 hours later, and start the plan that will change your body and your life.

DOUG GLEICHER

POUNDS LOST

15

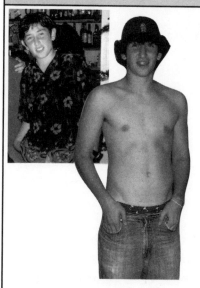

HEIGHT: 5'10"
AGE: 13
ABOUT DOUG: New York City native and athlete

"When I was a young kid, I was overweight and not athletic. The other kids in school called me fat all the time, and I hated it. When we had to run in gym class, I huffed and puffed my way around the track.

"My mom always worried about me, and she did everything she could to help me. She bought healthy foods, but my problem was how much I ate. I would just fill up my stomach with food. I ate so much that sometimes I felt like I was going to puke. I discovered that even if you eat healthy food, you're going to get fat if you eat too much of it.

"Now, everything has changed. Since meeting Jorge, my life is totally different. I lost 15 pounds of fat and probably gained about 15 pounds of muscle. No one calls me fat anymore. As you can see in my picture, I work out and play sports. I am only thirteen years old, but one of my dreams is to be a professional athlete someday.

"I now have a strong foundation for a healthy future, and I have what I've always wanted—a fit, healthy body that lets me do anything I want to do. My confidence is higher than ever, and I feel great.

continued

"Thank you, Jorge, for all your support!"

DOUG'S SECRETS TO SUCCESS

▶ Never skip breakfast! Jorge taught me that breakfast is the most important meal of the day. Breakfast doesn't have to be fancy, just make sure you eat it!

▶ Add exercise to speed up your success. I used Jorge's 8 Minute Moves® and they work great. Strength training exercises like the 8 Minute Moves® really build muscle and burn fat.

▶ One of my favorite snacks is a whey protein shake. One scoop of whey protein powder mixed with water is only about 100 calories. It will lower your hunger and help you build muscle.

14-DAY PLANNER

JORGE-ISM

" The power of support can help you overcome emotional eating. If you have a network of friends, you can turn to them instead of the fridge or cupboard. **"**

VISUALIZATION

Today you are going to take a journey one year into the future. Close your eyes and take a few deep, relaxing breaths. You are getting ready to attend a formal dance at school with the guy or girl you've had a crush on forever.

See yourself pull the long, slinky dress out of your closet or admire your tuxedo. Drape your clothes over a chair and take a good look. How do you think you will look all dressed up for the special event? How do you think your outfit will feel on your now-slimmer body?

Pull on your clothes and feel the fabric fall around your body. Notice how your dress or tuxedo fits, how no part of it bunches or grabs. It's perfect. Notice your slender arms and how shapely your shoulders are. Turn around and take in your rear view. How do you look? How do you feel?

Now, see yourself a few hours later, dancing with your friends at a beautifully decorated hotel. Notice how all eyes are on you, admiring how you look. See a smile creep across your face. You've reached your goal and you look fantastic.

Your 3-Hour Plan

- Commit your eating times (left column).

- Create your custom meal from the lists starting on page 172 or from the recipes starting on page 144.

- Check off boxes when done eating.

TIME	MEAL	SELECTION	X
___:___	BREAKFAST	_____	◯
___:___	SNACK	_____	◯
___:___	LUNCH	_____	◯
___:___	SNACK	_____	◯
___:___	DINNER	_____	◯
___:___	TREAT	_____	◯
	WATER:	◯ ◯ ◯ ◯ ◯ ◯ ◯ ◯	

If you weigh 200 to 249 lbs = double snack; 250 to 299 lbs = triple snack; 300+ lbs = quadruple snack

* Visit www.3hourdiet.com for an online version of this meal planner.

DAILY TIP

Develop a rotating menu system: To assist with meal planning and save time, plan out two weeks' worth of meals, snacks, and treats and then just re-use the same plan every two weeks. You'll save hours trying to brainstorm new meal combinations.

JOURNAL NOTES

JORGE-ISM

" Many people are too hard on themselves when trying to lose weight. Be patient. The weight will come off. It might not come off overnight, but it will come off. **"**

VISUALIZATION

During today's visualization, you will imagine a whole day's worth of your favorite healthy food choices. So close your eyes and take a few deep, relaxing breaths, in through your nose and out through your mouth.

You've woken up and gotten out of bed. Now you're heading to the kitchen for breakfast. What will you ask your parents to fix for you? Will you ask for scrambled egg whites, a piece of whole-grain toast with a little butter, and an orange? Will you ask for a cup of green tea? Decide what you will eat that will give you the energy and nutrients that your body needs to get you through the morning. Three hours later, it's time for a snack. Will you have a cup of yogurt or some string cheese? What about for lunch? Have you packed a warm, filling thermos of soup or maybe a delicious, veggie-stuffed sandwich? What will you enjoy for your afternoon snack? A crisp apple or maybe some fiber-rich crackers? Three hours later, you've got a dinner date. Decide which veggies will fill your plate. What else will you have? And then of course, you have a special treat, possibly a Hershey's Kiss®. Imagine yourself eating and enjoying each meal. Remember, food is fuel and your body feels so great when you give it what it needs.

Your 3-Hour Plan

- Commit your eating times (left column).

- Create your custom meal from the lists starting on page 172 or from the recipes starting on page 144.

- Check off boxes when done eating.

TIME	MEAL	SELECTION	X
:	BREAKFAST		☐
:	SNACK		☐
:	LUNCH		☐
:	SNACK		☐
:	DINNER		☐
:	TREAT		☐
	WATER:	☐ ☐ ☐ ☐ ☐ ☐ ☐ ☐	

If you weigh 200 to 249 lbs = double snack; 250 to 299 lbs = triple snack; 300+ lbs = quadruple snack

DAILY TIP

Try to keep breakfast simple: There are many quick, healthful breakfast foods available, so you can save time and energy by keeping this meal relatively simple. Stick with things like high-fiber cereal, whole-grain toast, oatmeal, and fruit—things you can throw together in just a few minutes. Then concentrate harder on your lunches and dinners.

JOURNAL NOTES

JORGE-ISM

" Once you get used to eating every three hours, your stomach will tell you when to eat. Our body sends us natural cues all of the time. We just need to tune in and listen. **"**

VISUALIZATION

Today is a glorious summer day filled with sunshine and warm breezes. It's the perfect day to hit the beach with a friend during a very relaxing visualization exercise. Close your eyes and take a few relaxing breaths, in through your nose and out through your mouth.

You've just gotten off the phone with your friend and you've decided to go spend the day at the beach. You haven't been to the beach in many years, maybe even ever, since you're too embarrassed to wear a swimsuit in public. But now you've got a beautiful body. So slip on your swimsuit, flip-flops, and wide-brimmed straw hat. You and your friend sing along to a popular song on the way to the beach. Once there, you sink your toes into the hot sand and let out a deep sigh of delight. Doesn't it feel great? As you undress down to your bathing suit and spread out on your towel, you feel confident and beautiful. Experience the warm rays on your back and give your buddy a wink. She comments on how great you look and you reply with a heartfelt "thank you" and tell her just how great you feel. The two of you spend the afternoon gossiping on your beach towels, frolicking in the waves, and strolling the length of the water's edge.

Your 3-Hour Plan

- Commit your eating times (left column).

- Create your custom meal from the lists starting on page 172 or from the recipes starting on page 144.

- Check off boxes when done eating.

TIME	MEAL	SELECTION	X
:	BREAKFAST		○
:	SNACK		○
:	LUNCH		○
:	SNACK		○
:	DINNER		○
:	TREAT		○
	WATER:	○ ○ ○ ○ ○ ○ ○ ○	

If you weigh 200 to 249 lbs = double snack; 250 to 299 lbs = triple snack; 300+ lbs = quadruple snack

DAILY TIP

Watch your socializing time: We all love to spend time chatting in class or on the phone when we get home, but five minutes here and there can add up to hours once the day is through. Make sure your socializing time is spent wisely, and you'll be surprised at how much time you save.

JOURNAL NOTES

JORGE-ISM

" Sometimes we're embarrassed to tell others that we need support. Most people, however, are very helpful once they understand why you are trying this new way of eating, and they will help you get to your goal. **"**

VISUALIZATION

Today you will use the power of visualization to help overcome negative feelings that can lead to overeating. You can use this visualization any time you feel a negative mood coming on. Use it whenever you find a negative emotion causing you to think of food. Start by relaxing with a few deep breaths. Allow each exhalation to bring you to a deeper and deeper state of relaxation.

Once you feel deeply relaxed, you are ready to begin. Notice the state of your mind. Are you feeling any negative emotions? Do you feel angry, sad, depressed, anxious, or fearful? Each time you exhale, see yourself releasing these negative feelings out of your body. See your breath literally blow them away! Then, each time you inhale, visualize yourself breathing in positive emotions such as love, compassion, joy, and peace. With each breath, exchange a negative emotion for a positive one, and feel your body begin to vibrate with positive emotions!

Your 3-Hour Plan

- Commit your eating times (left column).

- Create your custom meal from the lists starting on page 172 or from the recipes starting on page 144.

- Check off boxes when done eating.

TIME	MEAL	SELECTION	X
:	BREAKFAST		○
:	SNACK		○
:	LUNCH		○
:	SNACK		○
:	DINNER		○
:	TREAT		○
	WATER:	○ ○ ○ ○ ○ ○ ○ ○	

If you weigh 200 to 249 lbs = double snack; 250 to 299 lbs = triple snack; 300+ lbs = quadruple snack

DAILY TIP

Avoid postponing important tasks: Don't put off things that you're not looking forward to doing. They will only come back to haunt you. Things rarely are more fun when you postpone them. Allow plenty of time for big, important jobs and make them less daunting by breaking them down into smaller tasks over time.

JOURNAL NOTES

JORGE-ISM

"" It's when you're at a state when you feel okay—you've lost some weight and feel good about your body—that you are most likely to give in to temptation. It's easy to think that one overindulgence will be okay. Stand firm and stick to the program. Don't give up until you reach your goal. ""

VISUALIZATION

Close your eyes and take a few relaxing breaths—in through your nose and out through your mouth. Smile and jump into the future with me. Visualize the day that you reach your goal.

See yourself jump out of bed on a beautiful, sunny Saturday morning. As you get dressed, notice how you look. See your new arms, legs, and torso. Go ahead and get dressed, making sure to pick that outfit you've always wanted to wear, but couldn't because of your weight. Notice how your clothes drape loosely over your body. Feel how none of the fabric hugs you or feels tight. Touch your body with your hands. How does it feel? Walk around. Notice that your thighs no longer rub together. Look in the mirror and see how extraordinary you look and feel. What quality about your new self are you most proud of? Smile. You've reached your goal!

Your 3-Hour Plan

- Commit your eating times (left column).

- Create your custom meal from the lists starting on page 172 or from the recipes starting on page 144.

- Check off boxes when done eating.

TIME	MEAL	SELECTION	X
:	BREAKFAST		○
:	SNACK		○
:	LUNCH		○
:	SNACK		○
:	DINNER		○
:	TREAT		○
	WATER:	○ ○ ○ ○ ○ ○ ○ ○	

If you weigh 200 to 249 lbs = double snack; 250 to 299 lbs = triple snack; 300+ lbs = quadruple snack

DAILY TIP

Avoid interruptions: If you just can't stop playing computer games when you sit in front of your PC, step away from it. If you just have to get some food preparation and planning done for your 3-Hour Diet™ and your cell phone keeps ringing, turn it off. The best way to dodge interruptions is to avoid them in the first place.

JOURNAL NOTES

JORGE-ISM

" If you do slip up, just get back on the program. You haven't lost the battle until you've quit. **"**

VISUALIZATION

Today we will nurture your inner motivation with a very special visualization exercise. During today's visualization, you will be reunited with an old friend who hasn't seen you for many years. So close your eyes and take a few relaxing breaths, in through your nose and out through your mouth.

See yourself pulling into the parking garage at the airport to pick up your friend. Take a quick look at your mom or dad and receive a warm smile in encouragement. As you close the car door, glance at your reflection in the window and smile. You look healthier and happier than you have in years! As you wait for the elevator, take a peek at your watch. You only have a few minutes until your friend's flight is due at the gate. You quickly head to the stairs and mount them two at a time. Feel how agile and strong your body feels as you quickly climb each staircase. Doesn't it feel wonderful to be able to move quickly without feeling out of breath? You make it to the baggage claim just in time to see your friend approach. She smiles politely, says "Excuse me," and brushes past you. She doesn't recognize you! You call her name and say, "It's me!" Your friend turns around stunned and says, "You look incredible! What have you done?" You smile radiantly.

Your 3-Hour Plan

- Commit your eating times (left column).

- Create your custom meal from the lists starting on page 172 or from the recipes starting on page 144.

- Check off boxes when done eating.

TIME	MEAL	SELECTION	X
:	BREAKFAST		☐
:	SNACK		☐
:	LUNCH		☐
:	SNACK		☐
:	DINNER		☐
:	TREAT		☐
	WATER:	☐ ☐ ☐ ☐ ☐ ☐ ☐ ☐	

If you weigh 200 to 249 lbs = double snack; 250 to 299 lbs = triple snack; 300+ lbs = quadruple snack

DAILY TIP

Don't be afraid to say no: Whether it's to a social event or an extracurricular activity, saying no is not a crime. There is no harm in turning down invitations or simply saying, "I'm sorry, I can't" in order to get food preparation or other necessary chores finished. If you plan appropriately, you'll have time for the parties and events you really want to go to.

JOURNAL NOTES

JORGE-ISM

" Many people are motivated by photos of their bodies, both positively and negatively. A photo of you at your highest weight ever—or at your lowest weight ever—may help inspire you to stay on track. Keep the photo in your backpack—somewhere where you will literally bump into it often. It will remind you of your goal. "

VISUALIZATION

Today you will strengthen your motivation by visualizing yourself in the future, after you have reached your goal. Today you're preparing for a very special date with someone you've had your eye on for the last year. So first relax by closing your eyes and taking a few deep, relaxing breaths, in through your nose and out through your mouth.

See yourself getting ready for your date. Who will be your date for the evening? How do you prepare? See yourself taking a hot bubble bath or a long hot shower. Then, see yourself pick out your outfit. Find something special in the back of your closet, an outfit that you've always loved but one that you refused to wear because of your body. Maybe it is form-fitting. Put it on. See how great you look in this outfit! Notice how the fabric touches against your toned skin. Look in the mirror and twirl around and smile at how slim and healthy you look.

Hear the doorbell ring. Open the door and see your date. Hear your date comment about how fabulous you look. What does your date say and how does it make you feel?

Your 3-Hour Plan

- Commit your eating times (left column).
- Create your custom meal from the lists starting on page 172 or from the recipes starting on page 144.
- Check off boxes when done eating.

TIME	MEAL	SELECTION	X
:	BREAKFAST		O
:	SNACK		O
:	LUNCH		O
:	SNACK		O
:	DINNER		O
:	TREAT		O
	WATER:	O O O O O O O O	

If you weigh 200 to 249 lbs = double snack; 250 to 299 lbs = triple snack; 300+ lbs = quadruple snack

DAILY TIP

Put things in good places: When deciding where to put something, ask yourself, "Where would I look for this?" instead of "Where should I put this?" If you think about a good spot for something ahead of time, you'll save the time spent looking under beds and tearing apart closets to search for it later.

JOURNAL NOTES

JORGE-ISM

" The only person who can stop you is you. "

VISUALIZATION

It's such a beautiful summer day out, so today you will accompany a friend and his dog to the park for a day of sunshine and playing around. Get ready by closing your eyes and taking a few deep, relaxing breaths, in through your nose and out through your mouth.

See yourself rubbing sunscreen onto your lean legs, firm arms, and smooth face. Being active is a way of life for you. Feel the enjoyment from deep inside that comes from spending the day outdoors being active. You straighten your visor, grab a water bottle from the fridge, and step out your front door just as your friend and his pup Kobe are crossing the street. You jog down your front steps to greet them and give your friend a big hug.

The three of you walk the mile or so to the park, talking and laughing the whole way. As you enter the park, you stop off at a water fountain to refill your bottle and take a nice, long, refreshing sip. "Ahhhhh, that hits the spot!" you say. You head toward a big open lawn. Your buddy and you throw a Frisbee® and chase Kobe around the park. How great does it feel to be able to run and jump and play?

Your 3-Hour Plan

- Commit your eating times (left column).

- Create your custom meal from the lists starting on page 172 or from the recipes starting on page 144.

- Check off boxes when done eating.

TIME	MEAL	SELECTION	X
:	BREAKFAST		O
:	SNACK		O
:	LUNCH		O
:	SNACK		O
:	DINNER		O
:	TREAT		O
	WATER:	O O O O O O O O	

If you weigh 200 to 249 lbs = double snack; 250 to 299 lbs = triple snack; 300+ lbs = quadruple snack

DAILY TIP

Always carry something to read: We all have those moments of downtime—waiting for your parents to pick you up after school, stopping for a cup of coffee at your local coffeehouse—when it would be great to have a good book or newspaper to dive into for a few minutes.

JOURNAL NOTES

JORGE-ISM

"If you say 'I will,' you will be committed to the program and you will lose the weight. If you say 'I hope,' you won't be committed, and you will probably drop out. Today, tell yourself 'I will lose weight' and 'I will stick to the program.'"

VISUALIZATION

For today's visualization exercise, you're going to feel the breeze run through your hair as you and some friends take a leisurely bike ride through your neighborhood. Get ready to hop on for a fun-filled ride! Close your eyes and take a few relaxing breaths, in through your nose and out through your mouth.

Picture yourself dressed in a pair of comfortable shorts and a nice, cool cotton T-shirt. You're doing a few stretches as you wait for your friends to arrive at your house. See yourself in a sky-reaching pose: standing tall with both hands reaching up toward the blue sky. Feel the stretch lengthening your spine as you take a deep breath. See your friends steer their bikes into the driveway.

You wheel your bike around the side of your house and think about how much fun it is to be able to enjoy a day of bike riding. See yourself buckle the strap of your helmet under your chin, secure your water bottle into its holder, and pedal your bike out of your driveway. You and your friends pedal along, talking and laughing. Sometimes you ride slowly and leisurely, and other times you pick up the pace and playfully race each other. You are totally carefree as you glide through your neighborhood, enjoying the scenery and the sun on your face.

Your 3-Hour Plan

- Commit your eating times (left column).

- Create your custom meal from the lists starting on page 172 or from the recipes starting on page 144.

- Check off boxes when done eating.

TIME	MEAL	SELECTION	X
:	BREAKFAST		○
:	SNACK		○
:	LUNCH		○
:	SNACK		○
:	DINNER		○
:	TREAT		○
	WATER:	○ ○ ○ ○ ○ ○ ○ ○	

If you weigh 200 to 249 lbs = double snack; 250 to 299 lbs = triple snack; 300+ lbs = quadruple snack

DAILY TIP

Set a time limit for boring tasks: For example, when it's time to pack your snacks in the evening, limit your time spent on the chore to 20 minutes. When that time is up, stop what you're doing.

JOURNAL NOTES

_____

_____

_____

_____

_____

_____

_____

_____

_____

_____

_____

_____

_____

_____

_____

_____

_____

_____

DAY 10

JORGE-ISM

"Fat is not the problem. It's a lack of lean muscle tissue. Lean muscle tissue is your metabolism! It has everything to do with lack of muscle use.**"**

VISUALIZATION

Today we will again jump into the future, to Thanksgiving Day after you have reached your goal weight. Close your eyes and take a few relaxing breaths, in through your nose and out through your mouth. See all of the wonderful, delicious foods on the table. Notice how you feel. Did you eat 3 hours ago, according to plan? Yes, you did. You don't feel famished, as you have in the past. You don't notice any cravings. You feel completely in control. Take your plate and fill it up with healthful options, dishing up reasonable portions. What did you put on your plate and how does it look?

As you begin to eat, notice that you still feel in control. Chew your food and taste every bite. Notice how much more slowly you eat when you are not famished. Notice how much more you enjoy your meal. Once you finish, place your napkin over your plate. Notice how you feel satisfied, but not stuffed. Others around the table are unbuttoning their pants and loosening their belts, but you feel completely comfortable. Congratulations!

Your 3-Hour Plan

- Commit your eating times (left column).

- Create your custom meal from the lists starting on page 172 or from the recipes starting on page 144.

- Check off boxes when done eating.

TIME	MEAL	SELECTION	X
:	BREAKFAST		☐
:	SNACK		☐
:	LUNCH		☐
:	SNACK		☐
:	DINNER		☐
:	TREAT		☐
	WATER:	☐ ☐ ☐ ☐ ☐ ☐ ☐ ☐	

If you weigh 200 to 249 lbs = double snack; 250 to 299 lbs = triple snack; 300+ lbs = quadruple snack

DAILY TIP

Carry a notebook around with you wherever you go: Slip a small one into your purse or pocket so you can jot down thoughts that come to your mind. Or if you get the urge to eat something you shouldn't during lunch at school, you can express your feelings in your notebook instead of taking them out on a cheeseburger and fries.

JOURNAL NOTES

_____
_____
_____
_____
_____
_____
_____
_____
_____
_____
_____
_____
_____
_____
_____
_____
_____

DAY 11

JORGE-ISM

"There are no bad foods. Eat whatever you want—whether it's pasta, bread, fruit, or steak. You need a combination of fat, carbohydrates, and protein to create muscle."

VISUALIZATION

Close your eyes and take a few relaxing breaths, in through your nose and out through your mouth.

Visualize yourself at your goal weight, starting your first semester at the college you worked really hard to get into. Your parents are helping you move your stuff into your dorm room. Imagine running up and down stairs, carrying boxes of clothes, books, and CDs. Picture your strong, lean legs, taking the stairs two at a time. You bring your last box up to your room and collapse on your bed with a sigh. You give your mom and dad a hug as they head home. As you look around your room, a small smile grows on your face as you think about the new, independent, exciting journey that you're beginning. How great does it feel to begin this stage in your life with confidence? Aren't you excited to meet new people now that you're proud of your appearance? Doesn't it feel great to be so light and carefree?

Your 3-Hour Plan

- Commit your eating times (left column).

- Create your custom meal from the lists starting on page 172 or from the recipes starting on page 144.

- Check off boxes when done eating.

TIME	MEAL	SELECTION	X
:	BREAKFAST		O
:	SNACK		O
:	LUNCH		O
:	SNACK		O
:	DINNER		O
:	TREAT		O
	WATER:	O O O O O O O O	

If you weigh 200 to 249 lbs = double snack; 250 to 299 lbs = triple snack; 300+ lbs = quadruple snack

DAILY TIP

Pack all your food for the week at once: On Sunday night spend time packing all your food for the week in individual bags—one for each day. By laying everything out and packing it at once, you'll save yourself five days' worth of getting the food out you need to pack and putting it away again. When it's time to leave for school in the morning, all you'll have to do is grab a bag and head out the door!

JOURNAL NOTES

JORGE-ISM

" Don't be disrespectful to your
body. Your body won't be happy
and you won't be happy. You
need to be a friend to yourself, be
nurturing to yourself, and be
loving to yourself. **"**

VISUALIZATION

Today you are getting ready for a Halloween party, and you must wear a disguise. What will you wear? Close your eyes and take a few relaxing breaths, in through your nose and out through your mouth.

See all of your old frumpy Halloween outfits in your closet. Pull them out and put them in a pile for the Goodwill. You need an outfit that shows off the new you! Take yourself to the costume store. It's time to go shopping!

Find a sleek Halloween outfit at the store and try it on. Perhaps you chose the Catwoman outfit or maybe even a Superman costume. Try it on and see how it shows off all of your good qualities. Notice how, for the first time in years, you are not embarrassed to show off your body.

Take off the outfit and walk to the register to purchase it. See yourself smile. You look fantastic!

Your 3-Hour Plan

- Commit your eating times (left column).
- Create your custom meal from the lists starting on page 172 or from the recipes starting on page 144.
- Check off boxes when done eating.

TIME	MEAL	SELECTION	X
:	BREAKFAST		◯
:	SNACK		◯
:	LUNCH		◯
:	SNACK		◯
:	DINNER		◯
:	TREAT		◯
	WATER:	◯ ◯ ◯ ◯ ◯ ◯ ◯ ◯	

If you weigh 200 to 249 lbs = double snack; 250 to 299 lbs = triple snack; 300+ lbs = quadruple snack

DAILY TIP

Stop procrastinating: When you put something off until tomorrow, you lose today forever. Procrastination is the easy way out; it has no benefits. You will not do something better if you put it off until the last minute.

JOURNAL NOTES

13

JORGE-ISM

"Make this plan enjoyable. You're going to do this long-term and be healthy for a lifetime!"

VISUALIZATION

For today's visualization, you will bump into a boy you used to have a crush on, someone you haven't seen in a long time. Take a few deep relaxing breaths, and then jump into the future with me—one year from today.

See yourself sitting in the food court of the mall with one of your girlfriends. You are both eating healthful meals. A guy a few tables over keeps looking at you and then looking away. You recognize him, but he doesn't recognize you. You point him out to your friend, and the two of you giggle over his confusion. Eventually he gets up and walks over to you and asks if he knows you from somewhere. You tell him your name and smile as he looks shocked. He tells you how wonderful you look. How do his comments make you feel?

Your 3-Hour Plan

- Commit your eating times (left column).

- Create your custom meal from the lists starting on page 172 or from the recipes starting on page 144.

- Check off boxes when done eating.

TIME	MEAL	SELECTION	X
:	BREAKFAST		○
:	SNACK		○
:	LUNCH		○
:	SNACK		○
:	DINNER		○
:	TREAT		○
	WATER:	○ ○ ○ ○ ○ ○ ○ ○	

If you weigh 200 to 249 lbs = double snack; 250 to 299 lbs = triple snack; 300+ lbs = quadruple snack

DAILY TIP

Get organized: You can't think clearly if your surroundings are cluttered. A messy desk or bedroom will hinder your ability to complete tasks like homework or chores.

JOURNAL NOTES

JORGE-ISM

"The biggest reason to do this is to achieve your goals and dreams."

VISUALIZATION

Many of my clients tell me that they are most likely to overeat when they feel worthless or "not good enough." Today's visualization will help you to overcome such feelings. Today you will cultivate your inner self-love. Close your eyes and take a few deep, relaxing breaths, in through your nose and out through your mouth. Once you feel completely relaxed, you are ready to begin.

See yourself doing something that you do every day. Perhaps you are at school. Perhaps you are at an after-school meeting. Perhaps you are out with friends or your family. Try to see yourself through the eyes of someone else, someone who really cares about you, such as a close friend, parent, or teacher. This person really cares about you and admires you. Feel the same admiration that this person feels as you watch yourself through your friend's, parent's, or teacher's eyes. Try to see all of the good qualities about yourself that they see every day.

Watch yourself from afar as your loved ones walk up to you and tell you how much they love and admire you. Watch your expression as they tell you about your good qualities. What do they say? Now imagine more and more people coming into the room and staring at you with the same love and admiration of your loved one. As the room fills with people, they begin to applaud, clapping for you!

Your 3-Hour Plan

- Commit your eating times (left column).

- Create your custom meal from the lists starting on page 172 or from the recipes starting on page 144.

- Check off boxes when done eating.

TIME	MEAL	SELECTION	X
:	BREAKFAST		○
:	SNACK		○
:	LUNCH		○
:	SNACK		○
:	DINNER		○
:	TREAT		○
	WATER:	○ ○ ○ ○ ○ ○ ○ ○	

If you weigh 200 to 249 lbs = double snack; 250 to 299 lbs = triple snack; 300+ lbs = quadruple snack

DAILY TIP

Carry emergency rations with you: You never know when you'll find yourself stuck in a situation—like an after-school conference—when it's not appropriate to eat. Encountering such a situation when it's the time of day for a meal or snack doesn't have to derail your success on the 3-Hour Diet™. Keep a supply of drinkable yogurts and meal replacement shakes or bars in your backpack, purse, or locker. Then, when you know that you'll be stuck somewhere longer than you intended, you'll be prepared to eat on the go.

JOURNAL NOTES

MAINTENANCE

Congratulations on finishing your fourteen-day planner! By now you should have lost about 4 pounds, enough to keep you motivated to continue this path until you reach your goal. You've done a great job developing healthy habits that will stick with you for a lifetime, but you're not done yet!

You're on the right track, and some of you may even have reached your goal already. Whether you've reached your goal or have 50 more pounds to lose, you still need a game plan. This chapter will show you how to stick with the 3-Hour Diet™ for life. This is critical to your long-term success. If you go back to your lifestyle from before the 3-Hour Diet™, the weight is practically guaranteed to come back on.

So make a promise to yourself *right now* that you will continue with your healthy new lifestyle. You'll be able to continue losing weight until your reach your goal, *and* you'll be able to sustain your healthy weight for a lifetime. This maintenance plan will be like a map to guide you through the journey of a lifetime.

Have More to Lose?

If you want to lose more weight, just continue what you've been doing. You can follow the same meal plan from your fourteen-day planner, or you can continue to create meals using the 3-Hour Plate™.

Your meals will stay the same—400 calories for breakfast, lunch, and dinner; 100-calorie snacks twice a day; and your 50-calorie after-dinner treat. I think it's a good idea to continue planning out your meals using some sort of a log, like your fourteen-day planner. When you have all your meals planned out like that, you're less likely to slip up.

To log your meals, you can continue using the fourteen-day planner you just completed and cycle through it again. Or you can go to www.3HourDiet.com for more variety. There is a weekly meal planner with hundreds of recipes and fast food or frozen meal selections. You'll also be able to connect with thousands of other teens just like you for support. The website is an excellent resource for losing more weight or maintaining your weight loss. You can even pick up my cookbook, *The 3-Hour Diet*™ *Cookbook*, for more quick and easy recipe options.

I encourage you to weigh yourself no more than once per week. Pick a day of the week and weigh yourself in the morning. You can document your weight loss much more accurately if you weigh in at the same time every week.

What About Plateaus?

Everyone experiences plateaus on a diet, even if you've been following the plan perfectly. To plateau on a diet means to reach a point where you're not losing any more weight, even though you think you're doing everything right. It's important to not let these little setbacks discourage you! There are lots of reasons why we hit plateaus:

You're Menstruating

Some of you girls may have just started menstruating, or you may have started a few years ago. You've probably noticed that you retain water, or get bloated, during that time of month, which causes you to gain a pound or two. Don't worry, because once your period ends, you'll weigh yourself to find that you really did lose fat that week. Sometimes girls tell me that they have a hard time sticking to their eating plans during that time. They have hard-to-fight cravings for chocolate or other sweets. If you slip up and eat a Snickers® bar or something, don't beat yourself up over it. Just get back on the program 3 hours later. Criticizing yourself harshly will only lead to more emotional eating, so give yourself a break!

You're Taking a New Medication

Some medications like birth control pills or steroids can make you retain water, which boosts the number on the scale. Others, like some antidepressants, can slow your metabolism and increase your appetite, which lead to weight gain. Usually, though, if you experience these problems your doctor can switch you to a different drug that your body tolerates better.

You're Eating Too Much Salt

Sodium also causes you to retain water. Even though you aren't gaining fat, it still sucks not to see the numbers on the scale going down. Keep your salt intake below 2,000 milligrams a day. Try using salt-free seasonings like Mrs. Dash® and read food labels. Processed foods like chips, canned soups, frozen meals, and cold cuts have tons of salt. Try to eat more whole foods—veggies and fruit, whole grains, fresh fish and meat—instead of processed foods to lower your sodium intake.

You've Been Exercising

If you've been doing your 8 Minute Moves®, you've increased your lean muscle mass, which could boost the number on the scale. This is good weight, so don't get discouraged! 8 Minute Moves® will add about 1 pound of muscle to your body every month. As I stated earlier, this muscle will rev your metabolism and burn more fat.

You're Weighing Yourself Inconsistently

I recommend that you weigh yourself once per week, at the same time on the same day. You weigh more later in the day than you do in the morning because you put food and fluids into your body throughout the day. Also, all scales are calibrated differently. Don't be discouraged if your weight is different on a friend's or doctor's scale. Just continue to weigh yourself consistently and you'll start to see that number go down.

If none of the above applies to you, it's possible that you're estimating portion sizes incorrectly or you're eating emotionally without realizing it. Try writing down every single thing you eat for a week to see if you're really eating what you think you are. Also, measure out your portions with measuring cups and spoons to make sure you're not eating too much.

Reached Your Goal?

Congratulations! I'm so happy for you. To maintain this weight, you have to continue your 3-Hour Diet™ lifestyle. Because everyone's metabolism works differently, I can't give you a one-size-fits-all program to maintain your success. Try the following experiment to find your maintenance range of calories.

1. Follow the same meal plan you've been following for one more week, and then weigh yourself. If you find you've lost another pound or two, double your snack size to 200 calories.

You can easily do this by eating four snacks a day instead of only two snacks a day. This will boost your daily calorie consumption to 1,650 calories. Then move on to step 2. If, when you step on the scale, you are the same weight as the week before, continue with the 1,450-calorie plan. If your weight has decreased, go to step 2; if it increases, go to step 4.

2. Follow your new meal plan for another week and then weigh yourself. If after one week at 1,650 calories a day you continue to lose weight, then raise your snacks to 300 calories each, for a total of 1,850 daily calories. If your weight is the same when you step on the scale, go to step 4.

3. Follow this new meal plan for one week and then weigh yourself. If after one week at 1,850 you continue to lose weight, raise your snacks to 400 calories each for a total of 2,050 calories a day. If your weight is the same when you step on the scale, go to step 4.

4. Stick with your new meal plan, weighing yourself on the same day every week. If you begin to gain weight, jump back to the previous week's calories selection. For example, if you are currently eating 2,050 calories a day but have recently gained a pound, jump back to eating only 1,850 calories a day.

Now you've found your maintenance range. You might find that you need to adjust this range in the future, depending on your age, lifestyle, or exercise level. Just keep weighing yourself every week to stay on track.

So there are your guidelines for continuing the diet beyond the fourteen-day planner. Stick to this plan to take off the rest of the weight or maintain your goal weight for life. Remember, you need to have a plan to be successful. Implementing these guidelines will keep you healthy, fit, and trim for the rest of your life.

PART **IV**
RESOURCES

Remember to always ask for permission from your mom, dad, or any adult in charge before cooking. Never cook by yourself. It's always a good idea to have an adult nearby, especially when using sharp knives, graters, electrical appliances, hot burners, and the oven.

* For more recipes visit www.3hourdiet.com.

Cabo San Lucas Frittata

SERVES 4 • READY IN 15 MINUTES

I made this frittata for my family when we visited Cabo San Lucas, Mexico, and it was a huge hit! If you don't like too much heat, only use half of each jalapeño, but do use both red and green. The white onion and red and green jalapeños make this frittata look like the Mexican flag.

Cooking spray

½ medium onion, thinly sliced

1 green jalapeño, seeded and minced

1 red jalapeño, seeded and minced

8 large eggs plus 6 egg whites

1 teaspoon kosher salt

1 teaspoon cracked black pepper

2 tablespoons chopped fresh cilantro

4 slices whole-grain bread

4 teaspoons butter

4 cups diced mango (about 3 medium mangoes)

2 limes

4 teaspoons chili powder

Preheat the broiler.

Heat a large nonstick skillet over medium heat and spray with cooking spray. Add the onion and jalapeños and cook until tender, about 5 minutes.

Beat the eggs and egg whites in a medium bowl with the salt, pepper, and cilantro. Add to the skillet and stir into the onion and jalapeños. Cook until the eggs are mostly set but still runny on top. Remove the skillet from the heat and place under the broiler. Broil until the eggs are set, about 7 minutes.

While the eggs cook, toast the bread and spread with the butter. Squeeze lime juice over mango and sprinkle with chili powder.

Slice the frittata into quarters. Serve each person one slice of frittata, one slice of buttered toast, and 1 cup of mango.

Mushroom and Spinach Breakfast Burritos
SERVES 4 • READY IN 15 MINUTES

Mushrooms and spinach are a delicious flavor combination in these light, tasty burritos. Gruyère cheese provides a rich, decadent bonus; when you use a strongly flavored cheese, like Gruyère or Parmesan, you don't need to use very much because the flavor is so intense.

1 tablespoon unsalted butter	2 ounces Gruyère cheese, diced (about ½ cup)
1 cup sliced mushrooms	1 roasted red pepper (jarred), drained and diced
Salt and pepper	
2 cups packed fresh baby spinach	Four 8-inch flour tortillas
4 large eggs	4 oranges
4 large egg whites	

Melt the butter in a large nonstick skillet over medium heat. Add mushrooms and sauté until golden, 5 to 6 minutes, and season to taste with salt and pepper. Add the spinach and sauté until wilted.

Beat the eggs and egg whites and add to the pan. Cook until bottom begins to set, stirring to scramble. Stir in the cheese and peppers. Taste for seasoning and adjust if necessary.

While the eggs are cooking, heat the tortillas in microwave, about 30 seconds.

Divide the egg mixture evenly among the tortillas. Roll into a burrito shape and serve with oranges.

Italian-Style Eggs "Benedict"

SERVES 4 • READY IN 15 MINUTES

Traditional eggs Benedict is comprised of a toasted English muffin, a slice of ham or Canadian bacon, and a poached egg blanketed with hollandaise sauce—a rich, tangy sauce made of butter, egg yolks, and lemon juice. Our version preserves the English muffin and poached egg, but replaces the ham with turkey ham and the buttery hollandaise with tomato-y marinara sauce. The result is a delightful, tasty, and healthy version of a classic breakfast.

One 10-ounce box frozen chopped spinach, thawed and squeezed dry	1 cup prepared marinara sauce
2 whole-wheat English muffins, split	1 teaspoon white vinegar
4 teaspoons butter	4 large eggs
Four 3-ounce slices turkey ham	4 cups sliced strawberries

Bring about 2 inches of water to a simmer in a large skillet over medium heat.

While the water is heating, toast and butter the English muffins and warm the ham in the microwave, 45 seconds to 1 minute. In a microwave-safe dish, heat marinara sauce to a simmer in microwave. Keep the ham and marinara sauce warm.

When the water comes to a simmer, add the vinegar. Break the eggs into individual ramekins. Carefully slide the eggs into the water. Poach 4 to 6 minutes, until whites are set but yolks are still runny. Drain the eggs on a paper towel and pat dry.

To assemble, place one buttered English muffin half on each plate. Top each with ham, spinach, and egg. Ladle ¼ cup of the marinara sauce over each egg.

Serve each person one Benedict and 1 cup strawberries.

BREAKFAST

Turkey Breakfast Wrap

SERVES 4 • READY IN 15 MINUTES

Egg whites provide the highest quality protein you can find. However, egg substitute approximates whole eggs better when scrambled, so give a product like Egg Beaters® a try and see if you like it. Egg substitute is made primarily of egg whites, with flavoring and thickening agents, and has no cholesterol.

Four 1-ounce slices smoked turkey breast, diced in ½-inch cubes	Four 6-inch flour tortillas
Cooking spray	Four 1-ounce slices Swiss cheese
12 large egg whites or equivalent egg substitute (about 1½ cups)	4 medium apples

Heat a large nonstick skillet over medium heat.

Add the turkey to the skillet. Cook until the turkey starts to brown, about 2 minutes. Remove the turkey from the pan and set aside.

Spray the skillet with cooking spray and place back over medium heat.

Lightly beat the egg whites in a small bowl. Add the egg whites to the skillet and cook until they start to form curds, 2 to 3 minutes. Return the turkey to the pan and cook, stirring occasionally, until the eggs are set, 3 to 4 minutes.

Wrap tortillas in a damp paper towel and microwave on high for 30 seconds.

Divide the eggs among the four tortillas, top with the cheese, and roll into burrito shapes.

Serve each person one tortilla wrap with one apple.

Veggie Sausage and Egg Sandwich

SERVES 4 • READY IN 10 MINUTES

Serve these fantastic veggie sausages and eggs between two halves of a whole-grain muffin. Whole grains retain the bran and germ of the grain and therefore provide more fiber and nutrients than refined grains.

4 Morningstar Farms™ vegetarian sausage patties	4 whole-grain English muffins, halved
Cooking spray	4 teaspoons mustard
4 large eggs, lightly beaten	3 cups strawberries or fruit in season

Heat two medium nonstick skillets over medium heat.

Add the sausage patties to one skillet and sauté until they brown and crisp, about 5 minutes per side.

Meanwhile, spray the other skillet with cooking spray. Add the eggs and scramble until they set, 3 to 4 minutes.

While the sausage and eggs cook, toast English muffins.

Spread the bottom half of each muffin with mustard. Top with one sausage patty and ¼ of the eggs. Add top half of muffin.

Serve each person one sandwich with ¾ cup of strawberries.

FISH AND SEAFOOD

Fish Tacos

SERVES 4 • READY IN 10 MINUTES

Mexican crema is a tangy cream that's naturally thickened by the bacteria in fresh cream. It's very similar to French crème fraîche and American sour cream, both of which are readily available and perfectly acceptable substitutes. Crema provides a cooling, soothing antidote to the spicy tomato salsa that tops these fish tacos.

FISH

1 pound meaty white fish, such as halibut, swordfish, or mahi mahi

Salt and pepper

2 tablespoons lime juice, about 2 limes

1 tablespoon olive oil

8 Mission® 6-inch fat-free flour tortillas

SALSA

4 plum tomatoes, diced

¼ red onion, finely diced

1 garlic clove, minced

1 serrano chile, minced

2 tablespoons chopped fresh cilantro

Lime juice to taste

CREMA

½ cup low-fat sour cream

2 tablespoons lime juice, about 2 limes

½ teaspoon ground cumin

2 tablespoons chopped fresh cilantro

Heat a grill or grill pan over medium-high heat. Season the fish with salt, pepper, and lime juice and drizzle with oil. Grill until fish browns on one side, 3 minutes. Flip and grill an additional 3 to 4 minutes until fish flakes easily with a fork. Remove from the heat and set aside.

Wrap the tortillas in a large piece of aluminum foil and place on the grill to heat.

Meanwhile, stir together the ingredients for the salsa in a small bowl. Season to taste with salt and pepper and set aside.

In another small bowl, stir together the ingredients for the crema. Season to taste with salt and pepper and set aside.

Unwrap the warm tortillas and divide the fish evenly among them. Top each taco with 2 tablespoons salsa and 2 tablespoons crema.

Serve each person two tacos.

Vietnamese Shrimp Lettuce Wraps with Two Sauces
SERVES 4 • READY IN 10 MINUTES

Plump, juicy shrimp and bright red bell peppers are encased in crisp, refreshing lettuce leaves in this homage to Vietnam. Two delectable sauces accompany these exotic shrimp lettuce wraps: a spicy peanut sauce adds richness and a piquant soy-based sauce adds a salty accent. Try adding Asian rice noodles for a twist. This meal is best served family style.

SAUCE #1

¼ cup creamy peanut butter

1 tablespoon low-sodium soy sauce

1 tablespoon chili-garlic sauce

1 tablespoon rice wine vinegar

¼ cup coconut milk

SAUCE #2

½ cup low-sodium chicken broth

½ teaspoon minced garlic

½ teaspoon minced ginger

1 scallion, thinly sliced

Juice of 1 lime

1 teaspoon Asian fish sauce

1 tablespoon low-sodium soy sauce

1 tablespoon sesame oil

1 head Bibb or butter lettuce

1 pound shelled and deveined cooked shrimp, without tails

1 small red bell pepper, cut into thin strips

1 cup matchstick-cut carrots

¼ cup toasted peanuts, coarsely crushed

¼ cup chopped fresh cilantro

For Sauce #1, heat the peanut butter in microwave. Stir in remaining ingredients. Set aside and keep warm.

For Sauce #2, heat chicken broth in microwave. Stir in remaining ingredients. Set aside and keep warm.

Decoratively arrange the lettuce, shrimp, red pepper, and carrots on a large platter. Garnish with the peanuts and cilantro. Serve the platter with two warm sauces. Each person can pluck their own lettuce leaves, fill them with shrimp and bell pepper, and add the sauce of his or her choice. Eat the lettuce wraps like small burritos.

MEATS

Carne Asada Tacos
SERVES 4 • READY IN 15 MINUTES (PLUS TIME TO MARINATE)

These beef tacos bring the flavors of Mexico to your table in a matter of minutes. Marinate the skirt steak the night before you plan to cook it for a truly deep flavor sensation. Skirt steak is usually used for fajitas, and it comes from the diaphragm of the cow. It's incredibly tender, juicy, and flavorful if it's cooked rare and sliced thinly across the grain.

1 pound skirt steak	1 tablespoon extra virgin olive oil
3 tablespoons minced garlic	
Grated zest and juice of 2 limes	Cooking spray
3/4 cup chopped fresh cilantro	Four 6-inch flour tortillas
2 teaspoons kosher salt	1 avocado, pitted, peeled, and sliced
1 teaspoon cracked black pepper	1 cup prepared salsa
1/2 teaspoon ground coriander	1 cup packed baby spinach
	Lime wedges

Combine the steak, garlic, lime zest and juice, 1/4 cup of the cilantro, salt, pepper, coriander, and olive oil in a large zip-top bag. Smush the bag until the steak is well coated.

Marinate the steak in the refrigerator for 6 hours or overnight. Let steak sit at room temperature for about 30 minutes before cooking.

Spray a grill or grill pan with cooking spray and heat over high heat until very hot. Remove the steak from the marinade and add to the grill. Cook for 2 minutes per side for medium-rare or to desired doneness. Remove from heat, tent with foil, and let rest for at least 5 minutes.

While the steak rests, wrap the tortillas in a damp paper towel and arrange salsa, avocado, spinach, cilantro, and tortillas on a large plate. Set condiments on the table so people can assemble their tacos themselves.

Slice the steak thinly against the grain. Divide into four portions and serve with the condiments.

Main Dish Pork Fried Rice

SERVES 4 • READY IN 15 MINUTES

Forget about take-out and make your favorite fried rice dish more healthfully and quickly than any restaurant. Leftover chilled rice is easier to stir-fry than freshly cooked rice, because the grains don't stick together. Try adding fresh scallions for a colorful flair to this festive dish. Swap out the pork for chicken, shrimp, or even tofu if you like.

1 teaspoon peanut oil

2 eggs, lightly beaten

Salt and pepper

1 pound pork tenderloin, cut into matchsticks

One 10-ounce box frozen stir-fry vegetables

2 cups leftover cooked brown rice, chilled

2 tablespoons soy sauce

1 teaspoon sesame oil

¼ cup chopped fresh cilantro

1 tablespoon sesame seeds

Heat a large nonstick skillet or wok over high heat and add the peanut oil. Add the beaten eggs, season lightly with salt and pepper, and scramble until soft curds form. Remove from the pan and set aside.

Lightly season the pork with salt and pepper and add to the skillet. Sear the pork for 1 to 2 minutes until browned. Remove from the pan and set aside.

Add the veggies to pan and season lightly with salt and pepper. Stir-fry the veggies until crisp-tender. Add the rice and stir to break up grains. Add the soy sauce, sesame oil, pork, and eggs back to the pan. Stir to combine and heat all ingredients through. Taste for seasoning and adjust if necessary.

Garnish the fried rice with cilantro and sesame seeds. Divide among four plates and serve.

PASTA AND PIZZA

Capellini with Shrimp and Feta Cheese

SERVES 4 • READY IN 10 MINUTES

Capellini—angel hair pasta—is the perfect shape for this shrimp dish. The long, thin strands complement the delicate sauce, fresh tomatoes, and salty feta cheese. For a change of pace, replace the shrimp with scallops or clams.

PASTA AND PIZZA

4 ounces capellini (angel hair pasta)	1 teaspoon (or more to taste) crushed red pepper
1 tablespoon unsalted butter	½ cup bottled clam juice
1 tablespoon extra virgin olive oil	4 plum tomatoes, seeded and diced
1 pound medium shrimp, cleaned and deveined, tailless	One 10-ounce bag baby spinach
Salt and pepper	½ cup fresh basil leaves, torn
1 tablespoon minced garlic	4 ounces feta cheese, crumbled (about 1 cup)
1 large shallot, minced	

Cook the pasta according to package instructions. Keep warm.

Heat a large nonstick skillet over medium-high heat and add the butter and oil. Season the shrimp with salt and pepper and add to the pan with the garlic, shallot, and crushed red pepper. Sauté until shrimp are about half-cooked, about 1 to 2 minutes. Add clam juice, tomatoes, and spinach. Cook until the clam juice is reduced by half.

Add pasta, basil, and feta cheese to pan. Toss until pasta is coated in sauce and warmed through. Adjust seasoning if necessary.

Divide among four bowls and serve.

Smoked Turkey Pizza with Red Onions and Sage
SERVES 4 • READY IN 20 MINUTES

Most grocery stores sell smoked turkey legs in the poultry cases. If you can't find whole smoked turkey legs, you can replace it with prepared rotisserie chicken.

One 12-inch prepared pizza crust, such as Boboli

1 tablespoon extra virgin olive oil

2 ounces shredded smoked provolone (about ½ cup)

8 ounces smoked turkey leg meat, shredded, skin discarded (about 1¼ cups)

¼ medium red onion, very thinly sliced

¼ cup fresh sage leaves, sliced into thin ribbons

1 roasted red pepper (jarred), drained and sliced into thin strips

8 cups mixed salad greens

½ cup fat-free salad dressing

Preheat oven to 450° F.

Place the pizza crust on a baking sheet and drizzle with the olive oil. Top with the provolone, turkey meat, onions, sage, and roasted pepper. Bake until the crust is crisp and the cheese is melted and browned, about 10 minutes. Remove from heat and cool for 5 to 10 minutes.

While the pizza cools, toss the salad greens with the dressing in a large bowl. Divide among four salad bowls.

Slice the pizza into eight pieces. Serve each person two slices of pizza with one salad.

POULTRY

Turkey Cutlets with Lemon and Capers
SERVES 4 • READY IN 20 MINUTES

I love this dish. Crispy, golden brown turkey breast cutlets are smothered in a tangy lemon-caper sauce that's finished with a velvety swirl of rich butter. The flour coating on the turkey is crucial to giving your sauce body, but make sure you dust off all excess. Otherwise, the extra flour will burn and make your sauce bitter.

1 tablespoon canola oil

1 pound turkey cutlets

Salt and pepper

½ cup all-purpose flour

2 garlic cloves, chopped

1 cup low-sodium chicken broth

1 tablespoon lemon juice, about ½ lemon

2 tablespoons capers, rinsed and drained

2 tablespoons chopped flat-leaf parsley

1 tablespoon unsalted butter

8 cups mixed salad greens

2 cups croutons

2 cups cherry tomatoes

½ cup reduced-fat salad dressing

4 ounces crumbled blue cheese (about 1 cup)

8 paper-thin slices lemon

Heat a large nonstick skillet over medium-high heat and add the oil.

Season the turkey with salt and pepper and dredge in flour. Dust off excess flour and place the turkey in the pan. Pan-fry the turkey until golden brown on both sides and cooked through, 3 to 4 minutes per side.

Remove from the pan and place the turkey on a paper towel-lined plate. Tent with foil to keep warm.

Reduce heat to medium and add the garlic. Sauté until fragrant, about 1 minute. Add the chicken broth and raise the heat to high. Bring the liquid to a boil, scraping the brown bits from the bottom of the pan with a wooden spatula. Reduce the liquid by half. Lower the heat and add the lemon juice, capers, parsley, and butter. Taste for seasoning and adjust if necessary. Return the turkey to the pan and turn to coat with the sauce. Reheat at a simmer.

While the turkey simmers, combine the greens, croutons, tomatoes, and salad dressing in a large bowl and toss to coat. Divide among four salad plates and top each with ¼ cup of blue cheese.

Divide the turkey evenly among four plates and top with sauce and two lemon slices each. Serve.

Barbecue Chicken Polenta Stacks

SERVES 4 • READY IN 10 MINUTES

Store-bought rotisserie chicken, prepared polenta, and your favorite barbecue sauce make these stacks a cinch to make in minutes. These towering stacks make an impressive presentation for guests, so pile them as high as you can! The scallions and cilantro make a beautiful garnish as well as a tasty flavor accent. Try this dish with sautéed mushrooms instead of barbecue chicken for an unusual vegetarian variation.

POULTRY

Cooking spray	1 store-bought rotisserie chicken
Twelve ½-inch slices prepared polenta	8 cups salad greens
Salt and pepper	½ cup vinaigrette dressing
½ cup prepared barbecue sauce	½ cup chopped fresh cilantro
	½ cup sliced scallions

Heat a grill or grill pan over medium-high heat and spray with cooking spray. Season the polenta with salt and pepper and grill until warmed through and lightly browned.

While the polenta is cooking, heat the barbecue sauce in a medium saucepan over medium heat. Shred the meat of the chicken (discard skin) and add 2 cups to the barbecue sauce. Reserve the rest of the chicken for another use.

When the chicken and sauce are heated through and the polenta is grilled, place one polenta slice on each plate. Top with some of the chicken and layer another polenta slice on top. Continue layering chicken and polenta until your have 3 layers of each.

Toss the salad greens with the dressing. Divide the salad among four plates.

Serve each person one salad and one polenta stack garnished with cilantro and scallions.

SALADS

Grilled Chicken Summer Salad
SERVES 4 • READY IN 20 MINUTES

This salad makes a beautiful presentation with its verdant greens, yellow corn, red strawberries, and orange carrots. While it might seem odd to add strawberries to a savory salad, they pair deliciously with the balsamic vinaigrette. Try this salad tonight . . . it might become your new favorite!

Cooking spray
1 pound chicken tenders
Salt and pepper
4 cups mixed salad greens
4 cups baby spinach, torn
½ cup corn kernels (thawed if frozen)
½ cup sliced strawberries

3 scallions, sliced
½ cup diced carrots
½ cup reduced-fat balsamic vinaigrette
4 ounces soft goat cheese, crumbled (about 1 cup)
4 small dinner rolls

Heat a grill or grill pan over medium-high heat and spray with cooking spray. Season the chicken with salt and pepper and grill, turning once, until cooked through, about 4 minutes per side. Remove from the heat and let rest for about 5 minutes. Dice into bite-size pieces.

In a large bowl, combine the greens, spinach, corn, strawberries, scallions, and carrots. Add the chicken and dressing and toss to coat. Divide among four salad plates and top with goat cheese.

Serve each person one salad with one roll.

Ginger-Lime Grilled Shrimp Salad

SERVES 4 • READY IN 10 MINUTES

If you like Thai food but don't like the heat of its characteristic chiles, then this dish is for you. This refreshing arranged salad combines elements of Thai cuisine, such as ginger, lime, and soy sauce, but doesn't contain anything spicy. This meal makes great leftovers too, because the shrimp are delicious hot or cold. Just make sure you toss the salad with the dressing right before you eat it, not the night before.

SALADS

MARINADE

1 pound large shrimp, peeled and deveined

2 tablespoons minced ginger

Grated zest of two limes

4 garlic cloves, minced

1 teaspoon kosher salt

1 teaspoon pepper

1 tablespoon extra virgin olive oil

DRESSING

2 tablespoons freshly squeezed lime juice (about 2 limes)

½ teaspoon grated fresh ginger

1 garlic clove, grated

1 tablespoon soy sauce

1 teaspoon honey

1 teaspoon sesame oil

1 tablespoon canola oil

Cooking spray

8 ounces rice vermicelli

SALAD

2 cups thinly sliced Napa cabbage

2 red bell peppers, thinly sliced

3 scallions, sliced

2 tablespoons chopped fresh mint

2 tablespoons chopped fresh cilantro

4 cups mixed baby greens

3 ounces peanuts, toasted and chopped

Combine the shrimp, ginger, lime zest, garlic, salt, pepper, and olive oil in a large zip-top bag. Smush the ingredients in the bag until the shrimp are well coated in the marinade. Refrigerate for 8 hours or overnight. Let the shrimp sit out at room temperature for about 20 minutes before cooking.

Whisk together the ingredients for dressing in a small bowl. Adjust seasoning if necessary. Set aside.

Heat a grill or grill pan over medium-high heat and spray with cooking spray.

Cook the vermicelli according to package instructions. Drain and toss with 2 tablespoons of the dressing; set aside.

Drain and add the shrimp to grill and cook, turning once, until opaque, about 2 minutes per side.

While the shrimp cook, combine the salad ingredients in a large bowl with the remaining dressing. Toss to coat.

Divide the salad evenly among four plates. Top each salad with one quarter of the vermicelli. Decoratively arrange the shrimp on each plate and sprinkle with peanuts. Serve.

VEGETARIAN/MEATLESS

Tuscan Vegetable Panini with Roasted Red Pepper Soup

SERVES 4 • READY IN 10 MINUTES

Pacific Natural Foods® has several excellent brands of organic healthy soups that come in resealable cartons. One of my favorites is the Roasted Red Pepper and Tomato. It's rich, creamy, and so flavorful. Try them all to find your favorite!

1 quart Pacific Natural Foods® Roasted Red Pepper and Tomato Soup

Cooking spray

8 slices reduced-calorie whole-grain bread

½ cup prepared hummus

1 cup packed baby spinach

2 canned artichoke hearts, rinsed, drained, patted dry, and thinly sliced

4 roasted red peppers (jarred), drained and sliced

2 plum tomatoes, thinly sliced

8 thin onion ring slices

8 large basil leaves

4 ounces goat cheese, crumbled (about 1 cup)

Heat the soup in a medium saucepan over medium heat until boiling.

While the soup warms, heat a panini press or grill pan over medium heat and spray with cooking spray.

Spread each slice of bread with 1 tablespoon hummus. Divide the spinach, artichoke hearts, roasted peppers, tomatoes, onion rings, basil, and goat cheese evenly among four slices of bread. Top with the remaining bread. Place the sandwiches on the grill and spray with cooking spray. Close the panini lid, if using. If using a grill pan, weight down the sandwiches with a heavy skillet and flip halfway through cooking. Grill until the bread is toasted

VEGETARIAN/MEATLESS

and vegetables are warmed through, 6 to 7 minutes total cooking time.

Serve each person one sandwich and 1 cup of soup.

Teriyaki Grilled Tofu with Grilled Asparagus

SERVES 4 • READY IN 20 MINUTES

Vegetarians will love this meaty teriyaki grilled tofu. The hot grill gives the tofu a smoky flavor that's balanced by the sweetness of the teriyaki sauce. Nutty brown rice and grilled asparagus complete this healthy, Asian-inspired meal.

Cooking spray	1 pound thin asparagus spears, trimmed
1 pound extra-firm tofu, cut into 4 portions and patted very dry	1 tablespoon olive oil
Salt and pepper	2 cups cooked brown rice
½ cup store-bought teriyaki sauce	¼ cup sliced scallions
	¼ cup chopped cilantro

Heat a grill or grill pan over medium-high heat and spray with cooking spray. Season the tofu with salt and pepper and brush with teriyaki sauce. Grill until the tofu is golden brown and heated through, 3 to 4 minutes per side. Remove from the heat and brush with the remaining teriyaki sauce.

Season the asparagus with salt and pepper, toss with the olive oil, and grill until tender and lightly browned.

Serve each person one piece of tofu, garnished with scallions and cilantro, one quarter of the asparagus, and ½ cup rice.

WRAPS, SANDWICHES, AND BURGERS

Chicken Cheesesteak Sandwiches

SERVES 4 • READY IN 15 MINUTES

Associated with Philadelphia, cheesesteak sandwiches are not typically considered healthy fare. However, we've significantly lightened this traditional sandwich by replacing beef with chicken and full-fat cheese with low-fat. Serve with a side of pickles and you'll enjoy this meal even more than the original, because you know that you'll be feeding your body something healthy.

Cooking spray	4 slices reduced-fat provolone cheese
1 pound chicken breast tenders	4 small whole-grain sandwich rolls
1 onion, sliced into ¼-inch-thick rings, rings kept intact	
Salt and pepper	4 cups mixed salad greens
10 to 12 hot or sweet pickled cherry peppers, coarsely chopped	½ cup fat-free salad dressing

Heat a grill or grill pan over medium-high heat and spray with cooking spray. Season the chicken and onion with salt and pepper. Grill the chicken until it is cooked through, 3 to 4 minutes per side. Set aside.

Grill the onions until softened and golden, about 2 to 3 minutes per side. Coarsely chop the onions and set aside. Reduce the heat to medium.

Line the rolls with cheese and place cheese-side up on the grill, until the bun is toasted and the cheese is melted, about 2 minutes. While the buns toast, toss the greens with the salad dressing.

Top the cheese-lined buns with chicken, onions, and cherry peppers.

WRAPS, SANDWICHES, AND BURGERS

Serve each person one sandwich with one quarter of the salad.

Turkey Meatloaf Burgers

SERVES 4 • READY IN 30 MINUTES

Turkey meatloaf is a delicious, lower-fat version of beef meatloaf, but it can take a long time to prepare. If you take the same ingredients and make patties out of them, instead of loaves, you can grill them in no time. These unique burgers contain a mixture of spices and seasonings that create a delicious aroma while they cook to tantalize your taste buds.

1 tablespoon olive oil	1 tablespoon extra virgin olive oil
½ red onion, finely diced	2 teaspoons kosher salt
2 garlic cloves, minced	2 teaspoons pepper
½ teaspoon crushed red pepper	¼ cup chopped fresh flat-leaf parsley
½ teaspoon dried oregano	1 pound ground turkey
½ teaspoon dried basil	Cooking spray
1 bay leaf	**TO SERVE**
2 cups packed baby spinach	4 tablespoons fat-free mayonnaise
1 egg	2 tablespoons Dijon mustard
1 tablespoon Worcestershire sauce	4 reduced-calorie hamburger buns
1 tablespoon tomato paste	8 slices tomato
1 teaspoon soy sauce	8 thinly sliced onion rings
1 teaspoon red wine vinegar	1 cup packed baby spinach

Heat the olive oil in a large sauté pan over medium heat. Add the onions, garlic, red pepper, oregano, basil, and bay leaf. Sauté until the onions are translucent. Add the spinach. Sauté until wilted and set aside to cool. When cool, remove the bay leaf.

While the onion mixture cools, stir together the egg, Worcestershire, tomato paste, soy sauce, vinegar, oil, salt, pepper, onion mixture, and parsley in a large bowl. Add the ground turkey and fold in gently, but do not overmix! Overmixing will make the meat tough. Divide into four equal patties.

Heat a grill or grill pan over medium heat and spray with cooking spray. Add the turkey burgers and grill until cooked through, 5 to 6 minutes per side. Remove from the heat and set aside.

Spread 1 tablespoon mayonnaise and ½ tablespoon mustard on each hamburger bun. Top buns with burgers, tomato, onion, and spinach. Serve.

YOGURT, SHAKES, AND SMOOTHIES

Protein-Packed Breakfast Smoothie

SERVES 2 • READY IN 5 MINUTES

This smoothie is a sweet, delicious, nutritious, and easy way to start your day. Vary your fruits so that each day your smoothie is different and refreshing.

1 ripe banana

2 cups mixed frozen fruit (pineapple, mango, raspberry, blueberry, and strawberry are all good choices)

1½ cups (or more) apple cider (natural-style)

1 tablespoon honey

1 heaping scoop protein powder

½ teaspoon vanilla extract

Combine all the ingredients in a blender and puree until smooth, adding more juice as necessary.

Divide between two glasses and serve.

Layered Yogurt Parfait
SERVES 4 • READY IN 10 MINUTES

Parfait means "perfect" in French, and that's what this is. Serve this appetizing, layered treat in a tall, clear glass so that all the food is visible.

1 quart low-fat vanilla yogurt	1 cup blueberries (thawed if frozen)
12 graham cracker squares, crushed	¼ cup chopped nuts
1 cup sliced strawberries	3 cups skim milk

Spoon ½ cup yogurt into each of four large wineglasses. Top with graham crackers and berries. Repeat with a second layer. Sprinkle with nuts.

Serve each person one parfait with three-quarters cup of milk.

DESSERTS

Chocolate-Covered Strawberries
SERVES 4 • READY IN 10 MINUTES

Chocolate-covered strawberries and cream—you'll forget you're on a diet when you indulge in this luscious concoction.

3 tablespoons semisweet chocolate chips	4 tablespoons nonfat whipped topping
12 strawberries, sliced	

Place chocolate chips in a small microwave-safe bowl and microwave until melted, about 20 seconds, stirring frequently. Place strawberries on a platter and drizzle with melted chocolate.

Top with whipped topping and serve.

Ladyfinger Parfait

SERVES 4 • READY IN 10 MINUTES

Bright blue blueberries turn this simple vanilla yogurt parfait into an elegant ending to any dinner.

4 ladyfingers	½ cup blueberries
1 cup fat-free vanilla frozen yogurt	

Layer one ladyfinger, ¼ cup frozen yogurt, and 2 tablespoons blueberries in each of four small glasses.

Serve.

Rice Pudding in Phyllo Crust

SERVES 4 • READY IN 10 MINUTES

Phyllo dough is a thin, flaky pastry that is often used in Mediterranean desserts and casseroles. Frozen phyllo dough is available in the frozen pastry section of most supermarkets.

Cooking spray	2 tablespoons nonfat whipped topping
2 sheets phyllo dough, thawed	1 teaspoon ground cinnamon
2 single-serving nonfat rice pudding cups	

Preheat the oven to 400° F. Spray four muffin tin cups with cooking spray.

Slice the phyllo sheets in half, fold, and line inside muffin cups. Spray the top with cooking spray.

Bake until just browned, about 4 minutes.

Carefully remove phyllo cups from muffin pan and place on a plate.

DESSERTS

Fill each cup with one half of each rice pudding cup, top with whipped topping, sprinkle with cinnamon, and serve.

Strawberry Shortcake
SERVES 4 • READY IN 10 MINUTES

You can enjoy this refreshing summery dessert any time of year. If strawberries are out of season, substitute unsweetened frozen berries.

2 slices (⅛ of cake each) store-bought angel food cake, sliced in half	4 tablespoons nonfat whipped topping
1 cup thinly sliced strawberries	1 teaspoon powdered sugar

Place ½ slice of angel food cake on each of four plates. Top with strawberries and whipped topping.

Sprinkle with powdered sugar and serve.

Jell-O Parfait
SERVES 4 • READY IN 10 MINUTES

Simple, quick, and easy to make, this colorful dessert combination makes a stunning picture on your dining room table.

4 store-bought, sugar-free Jell-O cups, any flavor

1 medium banana, sliced

2 store-bought, fat-free vanilla pudding cups

In each of four clear glasses, layer one Jell-O cup, one quarter of the banana slices, and one half of each pudding cup.

Serve.

Frosted Cappuccino Shake

SERVES 4 • READY IN 10 MINUTES

Feeling like a lift? Try this chilled hazelnut cappuccino. It has all the caffeine and flavor of your favorite coffeehouse specialty but with a fraction of the fat and calories.

2 cups chilled prepared hazelnut coffee	4 packets artificial sweetener
2 cups skim milk	2 tablespoons nonfat whipped topping
1 teaspoon chocolate extract	2 teaspoons cocoa powder

Combine coffee, milk, chocolate extract, and sweetener in a bowl and whisk until frothy. Fill four tall glasses with ice and pour the coffee mixture evenly in each.

Top with the whipped topping, dust with the cocoa powder, and serve.

Frozen Banana Ice Cream

SERVES 4 • READY IN 10 MINUTES

An alternative to dairy ice cream, this frozen banana concoction is great for vegans and lactose-intolerant individuals.

2 large bananas, peeled, diced, and frozen	2 tablespoons water
	½ cup berries

Combine the bananas and water in a food processor and blend until smooth.

Divide among four bowls and garnish each with 2 tablespoons berries.

DESSERTS

Apricot-Almond Meringue Sandwich Cookies

SERVES 4 • READY IN 10 MINUTES

Meringue cookies are made of egg whites that are beaten until stiff peaks form. Sweet, light, crisp, and delicious, you'll forget that these cookies are fat-free.

4 store-bought meringue cookies	¼ cup nonfat whipped topping
4 teaspoons all-fruit apricot spread	¼ teaspoon almond extract

With a serrated knife, carefully slice each cookie in half, like a hamburger bun, and hollow out the inside.

Spoon 1 teaspoon of the fruit spread to the bottom half of each cookie.

Stir the almond extract into the whipped topping and add 1 tablespoon to each cookie bottom.

Sandwich the top half of the cookie onto the bottom and serve.

VARIATIONS

Chocolate-Cherry Meringue Sandwich Cookies: use cherry fruit spread and add 1 teaspoon cocoa powder to whipped topping.

Vanilla-Orange Meringue Sandwich Cookies: use orange fruit spread and add ¼ teaspoon vanilla extract to whipped topping.

Minted Strawberry Meringue Sandwich Cookies: use strawberry fruit spread and add ¼ teaspoon peppermint extract to whipped topping.

Brandied Plum Meringue Sandwich Cookies: use plum fruit spread and add ¼ teaspoon brandy extract to whipped topping.

Baked Figs in Phyllo

SERVES 4 • READY IN 10 MINUTES

Figs are soft, sweet fruit full of small seeds and juicy flesh. In this instance, fresh figs are baked inside a sheet of phyllo dough, creating a sweet Middle Eastern–type dessert.

4 sheets phyllo dough, thawed	2 packets artificial sweetener
Cooking spray	1 teaspoon ground cinnamon
4 ripe fresh figs	

Preheat the oven to 450° F. Line a baking sheet with parchment paper.

Spray each sheet of phyllo with cooking spray and put one fig in the middle of each sheet.

Sprinkle each with ½ packet artificial sweetener and ¼ teaspoon cinnamon.

Wrap the phyllo up around the figs like you're wrapping a gift, and scrunch the top together to seal the package. Spray again with cooking spray. Place on the prepared baking sheet.

Bake until the phyllo turns light brown, 5 to 8 minutes.

Serve.

Fast Food > Frozen Food > Snack > Treat Lists

BREAKFAST: FAST FOOD

These selections are the healthiest options that best fit the 3-Hour Diet™ format.

Arby's® Sourdough Egg'n Swiss Sandwich
■ Add fruit.

Arby's® Bacon Biscuit
■ Add fruit.

Chick-fil-A® Chick-n-minis™
■ Order the 4 count.
■ Add fruit.

Del Taco® Breakfast Burrito
■ Add 1 cup 1% milk.

Hardee's Frisco Breakfast Sandwich
■ Add fruit.

Hardee's Hash Rounds (medium)
■ Add Breakfast Ham and fruit.

Hardee's Made from Scratch Biscuit
■ Add Breakfast Ham and fruit.

Jamba Juice® Berry Fulfilling™ (16 oz.)
■ Choose protein boost AND take 1 teaspoon or 4 capsules flaxseed oil.

Jamba Juice® Mango Mantra™ (16 oz.)

■ Choose protein boost AND take 1 teaspoon or 4 capsules flaxseed oil.

McDonald's® Egg McMuffin®

■ Add 1 cup 1% milk and fruit.

McDonald's® Sausage Burrito

■ Add fruit (apple is available at McDonald's®)

SUBWAY® Vegetable and Egg (breakfast sandwich)

■ Ask for EXTRA veggies.

SUBWAY® Bacon & Egg (breakfast sandwich) on Deli Round

■ Add fruit.

SUBWAY® Cheese and Egg (breakfast sandwich) on Deli Round

■ Add fruit.

BREAKFAST: FROZEN FOOD

These selections are the healthiest options that best fit the 3-Hour Diet™ format.

Amy's® Apple, Strawberry or Strawberry & Cream Cheese Toaster Pops (1)

■ Add 3 eggs, any style.

Amy's® Tofu Scramble in a Pocket Sandwich

■ Add fruit.

Easy Omelets® Omelet, Cheddar Flavor

■ Add fruit.

Eggo® Nutri-Grain® Low-Fat Waffles (2)

■ Add 2 eggs (or 6 egg whites) scrambled with water and 1 ounce of the cheese of your choice. Top it off with a piece of fruit or a cup of berries. Note: when preparing eggs in a nonstick skillet, use cooking spray to keep them from sticking.

Hot Pockets® Ham & Cheese

■ Add 1 piece of fruit and 6 ounces of 1% milk.

Lean Pockets® Sausage, Egg & Low-Fat Cheese (1)

■ Add ½ cup of low-fat cottage cheese and 1 piece of fruit.

Morningstar Farms™ Veggie Breakfast Sausage Patty

■ Add 1 cup of orange juice.

Weight Watchers® SMART ONES® English Muffin Sandwich (1)

■ Add fruit.

LUNCH/DINNER: FAST FOOD

These selections are the healthiest options that best fit the 3-Hour Diet™ format.

Baja Fresh®

■ Any choice of 1 Baja Style Taco (chicken, steak, or shrimp). Add side salad with a squeeze of lime for flavor.
■ 1 Fish Taco with Charbroiled Fish. Add side salad with squeeze of lime or lemon.

Boston Market®

■ White meat chicken quarter without skin. Add a bowl of clear soup or a side of steamed vegetables.

■ Small order of Roasted Turkey. Add 2 sides: New Potatoes and Green Beans.

Burger King®

■ Hamburger. Add side salad with fat-free or low-fat dressing or squeeze of lemon.

■ TenderGrill Chicken Salad. Add fat-free or low-fat dressing and a packet of crackers if available.

■ Whopper Jr. without mayonnaise. Add side Garden Salad with Fat-Free Ranch Dressing.

Dairy Queen®

■ Grilled Chicken Sandwich without mayonnaise. Add a side salad with nonfat or fat-free dressing.

■ Hamburger and salad with nonfat or fat-free dressing.

Del Taco®

■ 2 Chicken Tacos Del Carbon

El Pollo Loco®

■ 1 leg and 1 thigh of Flame-Grilled Chicken. 1 (6-inch) corn tortilla and a corn cobbette or fresh vegetables.

Fazoli's®

■ Chicken & Pasta Caesar Salad. Add reduced-calorie Italian dressing.

In 'n' Out Burger®

■ Hamburger with onion, protein-style. Ask for half order of french fries. Add mustard and ketchup instead of spread on burger.

■ Hamburger with onion. Use mustard and ketchup instead of spread.

KFC®

■ Chicken Breast without skin or breading. Add order of green beans or 3-inch corn on the cob with order of mashed potatoes without gravy; add pat of butter.

McDonald's®

■ 1 Cheeseburger. Add side salad with low-fat balsamic vinaigrette.

■ 1 Bacon Ranch Salad without chicken. Add a Fruit N' Yogurt Parfait with or without granola for dessert.

■ Egg McMuffin. Add 1 cup of 1% milk.

■ Premium Grilled Chicken Sandwich. Add a side salad with a squeeze of lemon for dressing.

Sonic®

■ Grilled Chicken Sandwich.

■ Grilled Chicken Wrap without ranch dressing.

Subway®

■ 6-inch Ham without mayonnaise. Salt, pepper, and mustard optional. Add salad with choice of a squeeze of lemon or Kraft® fat-free Italian dressing or order of soup. Choose from the following: Roasted Chicken Noodle or Minestrone.

■ 6-inch Turkey Breast without mayonnaise. Salt, pepper, and mustard optional. Add Veggie Delite Salad with choice of squeeze of lemon or Kraft® fat-free Italian dressing or order of soup. Choose from the following: Roasted Chicken Noodle or Minestrone.

■ 6-inch Deli Tuna Sandwich, open-faced. Add Veggie Delite Salad with a squeeze of lemon or Kraft® Fat-Free Italian dressing.

Taco Bell®

■ All items ordered "fresco style."

■ 2 Ranchero Chicken Soft Tacos.

■ Beef, Chicken, or Steak Enchirito.

■ Gordita Baja: Beef, Chicken, or Steak.

■ 2 Grilled Steak Soft Tacos.

Wendy's®

■ 1 Jr. Hamburger. Add a side salad with fat-free French dressing.

■ Spinach Chicken Salad without croutons. Add low-fat honey mustard dressing.

■ Ultimate Chicken Grill. Add Caesar side salad with lemon squirt in place of dressing provided.

■ Chicken BLT Salad without croutons, and Fat-Free French-Style dressing.

LUNCH/DINNER: FROZEN FOOD

Many frozen meals do not come with a large vegetable serving, so we have created the salads below for your enjoyment and to complete a balanced, nutritional meal.

For all Lunch & Dinner options choose from the following salads:

If cheese is not in your frozen meal, choose from the following selections of salads:

■ Add a large romaine lettuce salad complete with ½ cup of boiled artichoke hearts, ½ cup steamed green beans, and 1 ounce of Monterey Jack cheese. Drizzle with 1 tablespoon of low-fat or nonfat dressing, or use 1 teaspoon of flax oil with a squeeze of lemon.

■ Add a large spinach salad with 1 ounce of feta cheese and 1 cup steamed and sliced eggplant. Drizzle with 1 tablespoon of low-fat or nonfat balsamic dressing, or 1 teaspoon of flax oil with a squeeze of lemon.

If your frozen meal does include cheese, choose from the following selections of salads:

■ Add a large iceberg lettuce salad with 1 medium tomato (sliced or diced) and 1 cup of assorted sliced bell peppers. Drizzle with 1 tablespoon of low-fat or nonfat dressing or use 1 teaspoon of flax oil with a squeeze of lemon.

■ Add a large spinach salad with whole or sliced mushrooms and a sprinkle of radish slices. Drizzle with 1 tablespoon of low-fat or nonfat balsamic dressing or 1 teaspoon of flax oil with a squeeze of lemon.

Lean Cuisine® Café Classics Chicken Carbonara

Lean Cuisine® Four Cheese Cannelloni

Lean Cuisine® Café Classics Three Cheese Chicken

Lean Cuisine® Dinnertime Selects™ Salisbury Steak

Healthy Choice® Chicken Rigatoni

Healthy Choice® Flavor Adventures Roasted Chicken Chardonnay

Healthy Choice® Oven Roasted Beef

Healthy Choice® Roasted Chicken Breast

Weight Watchers®, Smart Ones®, Pepperoni Pizza Smartwich

Weight Watchers®, Smart Ones®, Four Cheese Pizza

Weight Watchers®, Smart Ones®, Lemon Herb Chicken Piccata

Weight Watchers®, Smart Ones®, Pepper Steak

Amy's Kitchen® Spinach Feta in a Pocket Sandwich

Amy's Kitchen® Stuffed Pasta Shells Bowl

Amy's Kitchen® Cheese Enchilada

Amy's Kitchen® Vegetable Lasagna

SNACKS

These snacks are all about 100 calories. Modify your snacks according to your weight.

Almonds (12)

Angel food cake (2-ounce slice)

Baby carrots (2 cups)

Baker's® cookie (www. bbcookies.com) (1)

Breadsticks, 4-inch-long (2)

Brownie, small (1)

Butterscotch (4 pieces)

Candy corn (20 pieces)

Cashews (12)

Celery (3 stalks with 1 teaspoon of peanut butter on each)

Cheez-It® Twisterz (12)

Chips, baked, tortilla or potato (¾ ounce or 15 to 20 chips)

Chocolate-covered almonds (7)

Dannon® DanActive—Blueberry (1)

Dannon® DanActive—Plain (1)

Dannon® DanActive—Strawberry (1)

Dannon® DanActive—Vanilla (1)

Dannon® Light'n Fit Creamy, all flavors (6 oz.)

Dannon® Light'n Fit Smoothie, all flavors (1 bottle)

Dannon® Light'n Fit Yogurt, all flavors (6 oz.)

Earthbound Farm Organic Snack Pack: Carrots with Ranch Dip

Fruit, 1 piece

Fudge (1 ounce)

Gelatin (½ cup)

GeniSoy® Soy Crisps (25)

Graham crackers, 2½-inch squares (3)

Granola bar, low-fat (1)

Gumdrops (1 ounce)

Handi-Snacks®, Mister Salty Pretzels n' Cheese (1 pack)

Heath® bar (1 snack size)

Hershey's® milk chocolate bar (1 small)

Hershey's® milk chocolate bar with almonds (1 small)

Jell-O® Smoothie Snacks, all flavors (1 snack)

Kellogg's® Special K® bar, all flavors (1)

Kit Kat® (one 2-piece bar)

Knudsen® On the Go! Low-fat Cottage Cheese (1 serving)

Kudos® with M&M's granola bar (1)

Melba toast (4 slices)

Mott's® Single Serve Cinnamon Apple Sauce (1 cup)

Mott's® Single Serve Strawberry Apple Sauce (1 cup)

Nabisco® 100 Calorie Pack, Chips Ahoy! Thin Crisps (1 bag)

Nabisco® 100 Calorie Pack, Kraft Cheese Nips Thin Crisps (1 bag)

Nabisco® 100 Calorie Pack, Oreo Thin Crisps (1 bag)

Nabisco® 100 Calorie Pack, Wheat Thins Minis (1 bag)

Nabisco® Ritz Snack Mix 100 Calorie Pack

Nature Valley® Granola Bar, all flavors (1 bar)

No Pudge! Fat-Free Fudge Brownie (www.nopudge.com) (one 2-inch square)

Orville Redenbacher's® Popcorn Mini Cakes, all flavors (10 cakes)

Oyster crackers (24)

Peanut brittle (1 ounce)

Peanuts (20)

Pecans (8 halves)

Popcorn, air popped (3 cups)

Potato chips, fat-free (15 to 20)

Pound cake (1-ounce slice)

Pretzels (¾ ounce)

Pria® Bar, all flavors, (1 bar)

Pringles® Reduced Fat Original, 8 pack (1 pack)

Pudding cup, fat-free (1)

Pumpkin seeds (2 tablespoons, shelled)

Quaker® Quakes Corn Rings, BBQ (15)

Quaker® Quakes Corn Rings, Cheddar Cheese (17)

Quaker® Quakes Corn Rings, Nacho Cheese (17)

Raisins (30)

Rice cakes (2)

Saltine crackers (6)

Sargento®, Cheese Dip & Sticks Snacks (1 pack)

Sesame seeds (2 tablespoons)

Sherbet (½ cup)

Skinny Cow® Fat-Free Fudge Bar (1)

Skinny Cow® low-fat ice cream sandwich (½)

Soda crackers (4)

Stretch Island Fruit Leather, any flavor (2)

String cheese (1)

Sunflower seeds (2 tablespoons, shelled)

Tofutti (¼ cup)

Tortilla chips, fat free (15 to 20)

Trader Joe's Low-Fat Rice Crisps, Caramel
   (14 crisps)

Trader Joe's Low-Fat White Cheddar Corn Crisps
   (20 crisps)

Uncle Sam Cereal® (½ cup dry)

Whole wheat crackers (2 to 5)

Whoppers malted milk balls (9)

Yogurt, frozen, low-fat or nonfat (½ cup)

TREATS

Eat a delicious treat every day. In general, they should be 30 to 50 calories.

Animal crackers (4)

Caramel piece (2½-ounce piece)

Cheese slice, reduced calorie (1)

Chocolate chips (½ tablespoon)

Chocolate-coated mints (4)

Cookie, butter (1)

Cookie, fat-free (1 small)

Cookie, fortune (1)

Corn cake (1)

Crackers, Triscuit® (2)

Cranberry sauce (¼ cup)

European chestnuts (1 ounce)

Frozen seedless grapes (1 cup)

Gelatin dessert, sugar-free (1)

Gingersnaps (3)

Ginkgo nuts (1 ounce or 14 medium)

Graham crackers (2½-inch square)

Gumdrops (2)

Hard candy (1)

Hershey's® Hugs or Kisses (2)

Hershey's® Miniatures (1, any kind)

Ice milk, vanilla (¼ cup)

Ice pop, made with water (2-ounce pop)

Jelly beans (7)

Licorice twist (1)

Life Savers®, all fruit flavors (3)

Lollipop, Life Savers®, swirled flavor (1)

M&M's® (¼ of small bag)

M&M's® Minis (¼ of tube)

Marshmallow (1 large)

Marshmallows, mini (¼ cup)

Miss Meringue cookie (www. missmeringue.com) (1)

Nonfat ice cream (½ cup) drizzled with 1 tablespoon Hershey's chocolate syrup

Oreo cookie (1)

Popcorn, air popped (1 cup)

Pretzels (½ ounce)

Prune (1)

Raisins (1 tablespoon)

Raisins, chocolate covered (10)

Reese's® Peanut Butter Cup (1)

Rice Krispies Treat square (½)

Ritz Bits® peanut butter (5)

SnackWell's® sandwich cookie (1)

Starburst®, fruit chew (1)

Stretch Island Fruit Leather, any flavor (1)

Teddy Grahams®, honey flavor (6)

Vanilla wafers (2)

York Peppermint Pattie (1 small)

Letter to Parents

Dear Parents,

Your teenager is about to embark on the most exciting and rewarding journey of his/her young life. The 3-Hour Diet™ is going to change his/her body, boost confidence, and open doors that may have seem closed forever. We'll need your help. Your help will give him/her an enormous advantage; he/she will be much more likely to succeed with your support than all alone. So what can you do *right now* to help?

1. Get to know the 3-Hour Diet™. Here's a quick overview for the 3-Hour Diet™ so you don't have to read the whole book: The premise of the 3-Hour Diet™ is that skipping meals is devastating to weight control. When you skip meals, your blood sugar drops, which makes your appetite skyrocket. When your appetite is out of control, you overeat, especially in the afternoon and evening. On the 3-Hour Diet™, your teen will eat six times a day—three 400-calorie meals, two 100-calorie snacks, and one 50-calorie treat—with 3 hours between each eating episode. Your teen will eat an average of 1,450 calories per day, based on height and weight. I've created a visual plate (page 42) that illustrates portion size and how much protein, fat, and carbohydrates your teen should eat.

2. Shop for healthy foods. Help your teen stay on track by stocking your house with healthy, delicious, fresh foods. There are frozen and fast food options if there is *no* time to prepare meals, but fresh foods are healthier. Ask your teen about his/her list of favorite foods that he/she completed on page 45 and try to have those foods on hand at all times. Take a look at the quick and easy recipes in the

Resources section of this book and prepare tasty, light dinners for the whole family. Keeping healthy foods in your kitchen will help your teen immensely.

3. Love your teen unconditionally. Give your teen as much love and support as you can. Listen to him/her if he/she is frustrated or depressed and don't criticize. Teens don't need to be nagged or reminded that they're overweight; they already know. They need loving support and encouragement to reach their goals.

Thank you for supporting your teen on this journey. If you want to lose some weight too, I encourage you to join your teen on their path to wellness. You can pick up my original *The 3-Hour Diet*™ book in any bookstore, and it's even in paperback now. Or you and your teen can join our online club at www.3HourDiet.com. Lots of parents and teens have lost weight together on our site.

You can contact me or my team on the website any time. I look forward to working with you to help your teen achieve the body of his/her dreams and change his/her life forever.

Let's get started!

JorgeCruise

Jorge Cruise

MORE SUPPORT TOOLS

THE 3-HOUR DIET™ AT HOME FRESH DELIVERY

Take all the thinking out of following the 3-Hour Diet™ eating plan. Imagine receiving three delicious, chef-prepared meals, two snacks, and one delicious treat delivered fresh to your door. Visit 3HourDietAtHome.com to live like a star today.

THE 3-HOUR DIET™ ORIGINAL BOOK

This is the book that started the revolution. A must for anyone who wants all the secrets to the 3-Hour Diet™. Includes more than 50 easy recipes, in-depth success stories, and an insider's look at fad diets, including how low-carb diets make you fat. Available everywhere books are sold.

THE 3-HOUR DIET™ COOKBOOK

Over 200 delicious recipes to help make living the 3-Hour Diet easy and yummy! Includes a 14-day meal planner.

THE 3-HOUR DIET™ AUDIO BOOK

Experience the 3-Hour Diet™ revolution direct from Jorge Cruise. On his exclusive audio program, he will walk you through the secrets of how to lose 2 pounds per week without any deprivation or fad dieting. As an added bonus, you will also hear actual success interviews with 3-Hour Diet™ clients. Get ready to boost your motivation and success to the highest levels! Available everywhere books are sold.

THE 3-HOUR DIET™ BOOK IN SPANISH

Jorge's edition in Spanish has an inspirational foreword written by TV talk show host Cristina from *El Show de Cristina*. This version is perfect for the Spanish-speaking loved one in your life. Available everywhere books are sold.

8 MINUTES IN THE MORNING™ BOOK SERIES

Want to accelerate your results? Then make sure to get Jorge's exercise book series. These toning and firming exercises are used at home to restore lost muscle, thus revving your metabolism even higher. And they only take 8 minutes a day! Available everywhere books are sold.

AOL'S DIET COACH

Jorge Cruise is AOL's exclusive Diet Coach. Visit AOL.com for exclusive interactive material from Jorge to keep you looking and feeling your best.

USA WEEKEND MAGAZINE

Visit usaweekend.com for each new "Fitsmart" article Jorge writes as a contributing columnist for *USA WEEKEND* Magazine. Access the archives for more inspiration.

EXTRA TV

Every month, Jorge interviews America's top Hollywood TV and movie stars to find out what they are eating to look camera-ready. Visit ExtraTV.com for more details and air times.

Notes and Tips for Me

Keep track of your favorite tips, recipes, and things that work best for you!

_____

_____

_____

_____

_____

_____

_____

_____

_____

_____

_____

Notes and Tips for Me

Keep track of your favorite tips, recipes,
and things that work best for you!

Notes and Tips for Me

Keep track of your favorite tips, recipes, and things that work best for you!

_____

_____

_____

_____

_____

_____

_____

_____

_____

_____

INDEX

coconut oil, 35
constipation, 31
corn oil, 36
cortisol, 23
Crock-Pot™, 20
Crystal Light water, 70
cucumbers, 37

D

daily planner, 76, 81–135
 maintenance after, 136–40
daily tips, 76, 83, 87, 91, 95, 99, 103, 107, 111, 115, 119, 123, 127, 131, 135
daily visualizations, *see* visualizations
dairy products, *see* milk; yogurt
Dakotah, 66–72
dehydration, 39
diabetes, 15
diets, *see* low-carb diets; 3-Hour Diet™
Dietz, William, 9
digestive system, 31
dinner, 25
 visualization of, 85
Doug, 74–75

E

egg whites, 34
egg yolks, 35
8 Minute Moves®, 47–50, 78, 139
e-mail buddies, 60, 63
emergency rations, 135
emotional eating:
 accepting yourself and, 54–59
 definition of, 46

L

LDL (low-density lipoproteins), 35
lemons, 37
leptin, 21
lettuce, 37
lifestyle, obesity and, 12–13
limes, 37
love, need for, 59, 188
low-carb diets, 31
lunch, 25
    visualization of, 85

M

McDonald's®, 13
macronutrient, definition of, 30
meal plans:
    after reaching weight-loss goal, 139–40
    for two weeks at a time, 83
    visualization of, 85
    see also daily planner
medications, plateaus and, 138
menstruation, 138
metabolism:
    boosting of, 22, 37
    muscles and, 21–22, 33, 116, 139
milk, 34, 35
Molly, 8, 66–72
motivation:
    how to increase your, 56–58
    visualization to increase, 101, 105
Mrs. Dash®, 138
muscles:
    creation of, 77, 120, 139